Suing for Silence

Suing for Silence
Sexual Violence and Defamation Law

MANDI GRAY

UBCPress · Vancouver

© UBC Press 2024

All rights reserved. No part of this publication may be reproduced, stored in a retrieval system, or transmitted, in any form or by any means, without prior written permission of the publisher, or, in Canada, in the case of photocopying or other reprographic copying, a licence from Access Copyright, www.accesscopyright.ca.

Printed in Canada on FSC-certified ancient-forest-free paper (100% postconsumer recycled) that is processed chlorine- and acid-free.

Library and Archives Canada Cataloguing in Publication

Title: Suing for silence : sexual violence and defamation law / Mandi Gray.
Names: Gray, Mandi, author.
Series: Law and society series (Vancouver, B.C.)
Description: Series statement: Law & society | Includes bibliographical references and index.
Identifiers: Canadiana (print) 20230570321 | Canadiana (ebook) 20230570372 | ISBN 9780774869171 (softcover) | ISBN 9780774869188 (PDF) | ISBN 9780774869195 (EPUB)
Subjects: LCSH: Sex crimes – Law and legislation – Canada. | LCSH: Libel and slander – Canada.
Classification: LCC HV6593.C3 .G73 2024 | DDC 364.15/30811—dc23

Canadä

UBC Press gratefully acknowledges the financial support for our publishing program of the Government of Canada, the Canada Council for the Arts, and the British Columbia Arts Council.

This book has been published with the help of a grant from the Canadian Federation for the Humanities and Social Sciences, through the Scholarly Book Awards, using funds provided by the Social Sciences and Humanities Research Council of Canada.

UBC Press
The University of British Columbia | Musqueam Traditional Territory
www.ubcpress.ca

Contents

Disclaimer / vi

Preface / vii

Acknowledgments / x

Introduction / 3

1 A Civil Law Primer / 17

2 The Gender of Reputation / 41

3 Sick and Silenced / 62

4 Campus Sexual Violence / 79

5 Is Anti-SLAPP Legislation the Answer? / 94

Conclusion / 112

Notes / 125

Selected Bibliography / 154

Index / 157

Disclaimer

Borrowing from Joanna Bourke, in this book the central facet of what constitutes sexual violence is whether a person identifies what happened to them as a negative experience that was sexual in nature and unwanted, coerced, or not consensual, however they want to define those terms.[1] Therefore, if someone – either in the news, case law, or my research – identified their experience as sexual violence, I accepted their claim. This definition of sexual violence does not claim normative status, nor does it claim to be "truth"; rather, there is neutrality regarding the veracity of any claim.[2] Such an approach allows us to problematize a particular element of the issue: defamation lawsuits that follow the disclosure or report of sexual violence. The intention here is not to examine or make a judgment about the truth of the claim; the purpose is to examine the consequences of litigation, or the threat of litigation, for making statements about sexual violence.

Every man named in this book has denied the allegations of sexual and gendered violence made against him. A majority have resorted to legal action to vindicate their reputations, with varying degrees of success. This book is not about any single individual; it is a systematic examination of defamation law and the institutional structures that contribute to the silencing of sexual violence discourse. Canadian defamation laws, as this book demonstrates, do little, if anything, to protect those who speak publicly about sexual violence.

Preface

I became interested in institutional responses to sexual violence in 2015 after I reported a sexual assault to the Toronto police and the university where I was a first-year PhD student. My experience fuelled my desire to expose the disconnect between what these institutions publicly say will happen when someone reports sexual violence and what actually happens. This disconnect thrust me into activism, motivated by the naive assumption that these institutions would do better if they were made aware of the gaps in their policies and processes.[1]

Shortly after I went public, I received messages from women who wanted to tell me about their own experiences of reporting sexual violence. Rarely did these stories conclude in a way that the women found empowering. The women often walked away feeling traumatized and betrayed by the institutions they'd entrusted to support them.

In 2017, two of these women's stories took me aback. They were unknown to one another and lived in different provinces, but within several weeks of each other, they disclosed that they'd been sued by the men they'd reported for sexual violence. I asked Toronto-based civil litigator Joanna Birenbaum, who specializes in sexual violence cases, if she was aware of such lawsuits. She was, in fact, representing several women being sued for reporting sexual violence. At the time, I was unaware that this was a possibility. Prior to beginning my advocacy work in 2015, I'd asked an expert in the sector about the possibility of being sued. She assured me that if I'd made a formal report to the police and believed my allegations to be true, I was protected from legal action. This information was only slightly accurate.

A lack of awareness about such lawsuits within the antiviolence movement gave birth to the idea for this book. But on October 29, 2018, my research became personal in a way I didn't anticipate. That morning, I learned from Christie Blatchford's column in the *National Post* that I and approximately twenty others had been named defendants in a lawsuit initiated by author and (now former) University of British Columbia (UBC) professor Steven Galloway. I had not been served or sent a copy of the statement of claim. It wasn't until I logged onto Twitter that I learned what I was being sued for.

It was shocking to be named in a lawsuit, although the legal action itself wasn't unexpected. In November 2015, UBC announced that Galloway had been suspended pending an investigation into "serious allegations." Years earlier, like many women who messaged me during this time, A.B. (the pseudonym given by the court to the woman who reported Galloway) had contacted me for my insights on reporting sexual assaults in university settings. Following our conversation, she made a formal and confidential report to the university, and the university initiated an investigation. Following the investigation, UBC fired Galloway without severance, citing a "breach of trust."[2] An arbitrator decided that UBC's public statements violated Galloway's privacy rights, causing "irreparable reputational damage and financial loss," and awarded him $167,000 in damages.[3]

On November 14, 2016, more than eighty writers from across Canada – including Margaret Atwood, Madeleine Thien, and Michael Ondaatje – published an open letter on a website titled UBC Accountable and employed the Twitter hashtag #UBCAccountable to show their support for Galloway. They alleged the investigation lacked due process.[4] Atwood also released a statement about why she signed the letter in which she compared the Galloway investigation to the Salem witch trials.[5] This series of events prompted widespread (often hostile) debate on Twitter, to which I contributed. I also wrote an op-ed about Atwood's position.[6]

However, I used caution when tweeting about the case for two reasons. First, A.B. and I had become friends over the years. She never intended for the case to be in the media, so I chose my words carefully to avoid revealing personal information about her. Second, I had learned how easy it is to initiate a defamation lawsuit against an individual, especially if comments are based on second-hand information.

The statement of claim alleged that seven of my tweets defamed Steven Galloway. At the time of writing, the litigation is still before the courts, with no end in sight. Even though the tweets are now part of the public record, accessible to anyone who requests them from the courts, I am unable to replicate what was written because any reproduction of the tweets could make me vulnerable to additional claims of defamation.

I have tried not to let the ongoing lawsuit impact my writing or research, but if I'm being honest, I made the difficult decision to self-censor, not just because of the lawsuit currently against me but out of fear of future legal action from litigious men. I could not survive another lawsuit, financially or emotionally. I share this personal story because I wanted to be transparent about the experiences that shaped my research. At times, I reference the Galloway lawsuit. I want readers to be aware that I have personal insight into the proceedings and a personal interest in how the lawsuit resolves. But this is an academic study, so I have tried to leave myself out of the findings as much as possible to focus on the research participants' narratives and my findings. Readers can interpret the legal action against me and my perspectives in whatever way they see fit.

Acknowledgments

Thank you to Randy Schmidt, Ann Macklem, Lesley Erickson, and the staff and board of UBC Press for their ongoing support of this book. My thanks to the two peer reviewers who provided thoughtful feedback and helped to improve the work.

Many thanks to my mentors, Amanda Glasbeek and Amber Gazso, who helped shape this work from the beginning. Their guidance and mentorship have been invaluable. Joanna Birenbaum, a civil litigator and sexual assault law expert, has supported my advocacy work and my academic endeavours since the day I first met her in 2015. Joanna's expertise in sexual assault law was foundational for this project. I would also like to acknowledge Rita Henderson, a fabulous mentor who ensured that I was able to finish this book during my appointment at the University of Calgary.

Thank you to my fantastic lawyers at JFK Law who are currently representing me in my own defamation legal battle. Thank you to Karey Brooks, Aria Laskin, and Laura Edwards for your advocacy.

I'm grateful to have a supportive community who helped me grow as a writer, researcher, and advocate. Thank you, Amanda Hardman, Amrit Dhillon, Annelies Cooper, Caralea Cole, Caitlin Janzen, Chelsey Rhodes, Farzana Doctor, Glynnis Kirchmeier, Farrah Khan, Heather Bristow, Jessica Evans, Kelly Showker, Kristen Bos, Laura Pin, Mylene Inocencio, Nilum Panesar, Nora Currie, Sabrina Scott, Sarah Benson, Tamera Burnett, and Tobin LeBlanc Haley.

I am so grateful to all the silence breakers who shared many of their worst life experiences with me. I am honoured that you trusted me to tell your stories. Thank you to the anonymous silence breakers who spoke with me as well as Bonnie Robichaud, Constance Backhouse, Julie S. Lalonde, Julie Macfarlane, and Senator Marilou McPhedran.

Finally, thank you to my family for always supporting my academic endeavours.

Suing for Silence

Introduction

> Being sued nonetheless felt to me like a form of violence, a way for one person to strike at another by miring them in legal process.
> – Evelyn Lau, *Inside Out: Reflections on a Life So Far*

In summer 2017, I received a Facebook message from Lynn, a Canadian tattoo artist in her late twenties. Women from all over the world often sent me messages, to share stories like my own, about reporting sexual violence to the police, their university, or their workplace and being met with institutional betrayal.[1] Lynn had a different experience than those I typically heard. Several years earlier, Lynn had been working in France as an apprentice tattoo artist. Her mentor bullied and harassed her. Over time, the bullying and harassment escalated to repeated sexual harassment and, eventually, rape. Her work visa had expired, so she was working under the table, which made her especially vulnerable to his abuse. Eventually, she decided she could no longer tolerate his abuse. She reported him to the police for illegal employment practices and numerous instances of sexual violence. The police laid criminal charges. The case went to trial, and he was acquitted.

Unknown to Lynn, following an acquittal for rape in France, the accused can proceed with both criminal and civil charges against their accuser. Her mentor decided to pursue this option. But Lynn was back in Canada. She received a notice from the Canadian government, informing her that she was being sued and could face jail time for reporting the assault to the police. After a six-year legal battle, Lynn was acquitted of the criminal charges and the lawsuit was unsuccessful.

Despite the apparent legal victory, Lynn remained fearful of talking about what had happened to her. The courts deemed that there was not enough evidence to convict her mentor of rape, but they also decided that there was not enough evidence to determine that her allegation was false. Fearful of facing further legal retaliation, she was, effectively, silenced. There were other repercussions. She had to take time off from her art practice to travel to France for court dates, causing her financial problems and costing her professional opportunities at a pivotal time in her career.

At the time, I believed these types of legal actions were an injustice happening elsewhere, not in Canada. Later that summer, I met another woman who shared with me that she had been sued after reporting sexual violence. It happened in Toronto. Like Lynn, she told me that being sued instilled so much fear in her that she self-censored to the point where she even avoided having general conversations among friends about sexual violence.

I had no idea it was possible to be sued for making a formal report of sexual violence. At the time, within both the antiviolence community and feminist academic literature, there was a lack of discussion about the possibility of civil legal action for reporting sexual violence. Then, that fall, the viral #MeToo hashtag brought sexual violence to the forefront of global discussion.[2] Although the movement was heralded as a sign of progress for women internationally, the people encouraged by the movement to come forward experienced backlash. One mechanism of this backlash was the use of defamation lawsuits. Indeed, they became so common that the *New York Times* declared in 2020 that defamation lawsuits were the new legal battleground for litigating sexual violence cases: "Women and men on both sides of #MeToo are embracing the centuries-old tool of defamation lawsuits, opening an alternative battlefield for accusations of sexual misconduct."[3] According to the *New York Times*, plaintiffs were using defamation law for the typical purpose of dissuading speech that results in reputational damage. But they were also using it to "endorse their version of disputed events."[4]

In 2021, the United Nations released the *Report of the Special Rapporteur on the Promotion and Protection of the Right to Freedom of Opinion and*

Expression, which highlighted the global rise in defamation lawsuits, specifically against those who had publicly denounced perpetrators of sexual violence. It stated, "Weaponizing the justice system to silence women feeds impunity while also undermining free speech."[5] Evidence suggests that this is a global problem. Similar lawsuits have been reported by news media in countries such as the United States, Peru, China, South Korea, India, Australia, England, and France.[6] In the last five years, there have been numerous high-profile defamation lawsuits initiated by powerful men such as Hollywood producer Brett Ratner, Oxford professor Tariq Ramadan, businessman Robert Herjavec, CTV reporter Paul Bliss, poet Jeramy Dodds, writer Stephen Elliott, producer Chris Nelson, musician Marilyn Manson, and popstar Justin Bieber.[7] Famous women who have been public about their experiences of sexual violence have also been sued for defamation, including Taylor Swift and Kesha.[8]

The most notable defamation lawsuit to date is probably actor Johnny Depp's defamation action against his famous ex-wife Amber Heard. In 2016, Heard filed for divorce from Depp and sought a temporary restraining order alleging physical abuse.[9] A UK newspaper labelled Depp a "wife beater," which led Depp to sue the newspaper, a case he lost. The judge ruled that the newspaper was accurate in reporting that Depp had been violent in his relationship with Heard and referred to fourteen separate incidents. In the United States, in an op-ed for the *Washington Post* about how women are treated after reporting domestic violence, Heard wrote: "I became a public figure representing domestic violence, and I felt the full force of our culture's wrath for women who speak out."[10] Heard did not name Depp in her article. In 2019, Depp sued Heard for the article. In 2021, Heard countersued. In April 2022, the defamation trial began before a jury.

The six-week trial quickly became a public spectacle as the legal proceedings were livestreamed across social media platforms. Social media content creators took clips of the testimony to make fun of Heard while exonerating Depp. Each day of the trial, hashtags such as #AmberHeardIsALiar and #AmberHeardAbuser trended on social media.[11] Depp supporters globally harassed and attacked anyone who supported Heard or questioned Depp's claims of innocence.[12] The jurors ruled that both Depp and Heard were liable for defamation. They awarded Depp $15 million in damages, and Heard $2 million. Heard appealed the decision, which was settled in December 2022. She released a public statement declaring that she'd decided to settle because she'd lost faith in the American legal system, a system in which her "unprotected testimony served as entertainment and social media fodder."[13]

The legal action against Heard, coupled with social media commentary, made a loud statement to people who have experienced sexual violence and those who will experience sexual violence in the years to come: keep quiet or risk serious legal action and social consequences. The more privileged and powerful the man, the more severe the consequences, as these men can harass and abuse with impunity.

While defamation lawsuits tend to be a tool for powerful, rich, and famous men, it is important to stress that they are not the only men who initiate them. Given the resources required to initiate legal action, the men are typically well resourced, but not necessarily famous or wealthy. Nor is it only white, privileged, celebrity women who are being sued. Such cases are simply more likely to be reported by the media. The TIME's Up Legal Defense Fund, initiated following #MeToo to support Americans who have experienced workplace sexual violence, reported that 33 of the 193 cases they were supporting involved workers who came forward and were then sued for defamation.[14] Many defendants in these legal actions are not privileged and do not have access to the financial resources necessary for legal representation. Access to legal representation is further complicated for survivors experiencing intersecting forms of structural marginalization such as racism, colonialism, ableism, and homophobia.

This book focuses on the experiences of Canadian women who have been sued or threatened with a lawsuit for disclosing or reporting sexual violence or supporting someone who had experienced sexual violence. The research was guided by three central questions: What are the consequences of defamation lawsuits at both the individual and societal levels? To what extent are these lawsuits silencing public discourse about sexual violence? And, finally, are they strategic lawsuits against public participation (SLAPPs)?[15]

The book demonstrates that abusive men can strategically use defamation law to silence accusations of sexual violence and recast themselves as the "true victims" of "false allegations." When abusive men take legal action against their accusers, the action provides a legitimate avenue, such as the courts, to continue their abusive behaviour. This is not to suggest that men who have been falsely accused of sexual violence should be denied the ability to vindicate their reputations; rather, we must keep in mind that while false accusations do occur, they are incredibly rare.[16]

In Canada, there is a low threshold for what constitutes a defamatory statement: as long as a communication "would cause the plaintiff to lose respect or esteem in the eyes of others," that communication can be cause for a defamation lawsuit.[17] Therefore, the law of defamation often works in favour of the plaintiff – the person who initiated the lawsuit – because it puts the onus on the defendant to justify their statements, a task that has particular challenges in sexual violence cases, particularly in a legal system demonstrably shaped by discriminatory rape myths.

I employ Jennifer Freyd's concept of DARVO (deny, attack, and reverse victim and offender) to understand men's motivation for initiating defamation lawsuits.[18] This concept captures the disingenuous ways that abusive men make use of legal mechanisms to represent themselves as victims while undermining the credibility of the women who have called them out for their abusive behaviour. Abusive men will often threaten defamation lawsuits and make false accusations against the individual who confronted them to further situate themselves as the victims of an unfair attack. This is done strategically to create the impression that they are the real victim and the person who has made the complaint about their behaviour is the offender. The more actions that are taken to hold the offender accountable, the more victimhood the abuser can claim.[19] Freyd acknowledges that men who are innocent will defend themselves against false allegations, but it is abusive men who engage numerous forms of retaliation against their accusers to shift the narrative away from the allegations and toward an investigation into their victimhood because of false allegations.

The Myth of False Accusations as a Common Occurrence

As the #MeToo movement gained traction, a loud antifeminist backlash took over. The countermovement centred white male victimhood by claiming false accusations had victimized these men. It successfully shifted the focus from experiences of gendered violence to the inaccurate notion that men should be worried about being falsely accused of sexual violence.[20]

For example, the counterhashtag #HimToo rose to prominence after a woman tweeted that the #MeToo movement had resulted in her son no longer going on dates with women alone "due to the current climate of false sexual accusations by radical feminists with an axe to grind."[21] The #HimToo hashtag recirculated after Dr. Christine Blasey Ford came forward with allegations of sexual violence against US Supreme Court nominee Brett Kavanaugh.[22] Media pundits and politicians, including former US president Donald Trump, expressed concern that men's lives were being unfairly destroyed by false allegations of sexual violence.[23] Canadian media pundits similarly linked male victimhood to false allegations.[24] These perspectives perpetuate the harmful myth that false allegations are common and that protecting men's reputations should take priority over addressing the pervasive and global issue of sexual violence. These perspectives also tend to see an acquittal or an inconclusive investigative finding as evidence of a false allegation. According to law professor Constance Backhouse,

> "Not guilty" does not mean you are innocent. It means that the Crown could not prove your guilt beyond a reasonable doubt. And as we know in a sexist legal system, individuals accused of sexual crimes may quite often be guilty, yet the prosecutor is unable to prove it to a jury and judge beyond a reasonable doubt. Trial judges will often say, "I believe the complainant, but the evidence still leaves me with a reasonable doubt regarding the conviction." Our criminal justice system is quite capable of interpreting the Criminal Code in a sexist way. Consequently, it doesn't follow that after an acquittal anyone should proclaim that the complainant "lied." It does not follow. It is not the same thing. It seems to me that we should be careful about allowing the accused to claim, "I'm innocent."[25]

The problem is that there's no agreement on what constitutes a false allegation. According to psychologist David Lisak, the most comprehensive and accurate definition of a false allegation of sexual assault comes from the International Association of Chiefs of Police:

> The determination that a report of sexual assault is false can be made only if the evidence establishes that no crime was committed or

attempted. *This determination can be made only after a thorough investigation.* This should not be confused with an investigation that fails to prove a sexual assault occurred. In that case the investigation would be labeled unsubstantiated. *The determination that a report is false must be supported by evidence that the assault did not happen.*[26]

Despite the clarity in this definition, the line between a false accusation and the absence of evidence to substantiate a claim of sexual violence is often blurred in practice. Media and popular discourses tend to conflate false allegations with acquittals and cases unproven by police or campus investigations in a self-perpetuating cycle that keeps the myth that women frequently lie about sexual violence alive. The corollary to this widespread myth is that men and their reputations are the victims of women's mendacity. Assumptions about women's capacity to lie are also intertwined with stereotypes about race, gender, and sexuality.[27] The narratives of survivors who experience intersecting forms of structural marginalization are regarded as less credible.

Canadian feminist antiviolence advocates have long recognized that the police's tendency to declare women's accusations unfounded is a major barrier to reporting. The frequency with which police dismiss claims of sexual assault came to the public's attention when journalist Robyn Doolittle, investigating for the *Globe and Mail,* found that police dismiss sexual assault reports more than any other crime.[28] The Canadian Centre for Justice Statistics Policing Services Program states that an "incident is 'unfounded' if it has been determined that no violations of the law took place at that time or location."[29] Doolittle found that nearly one in five reports of sexual assault are deemed unfounded in Canada. This is nearly double the rate for physical assault and dramatically higher than the rates for all other crimes.[30] When unfounded cases are considered part of the total count of sexual assault charges reported, only 34 percent of such reports result in charges being laid.[31] This staggering rate of dismissal by police, acting as gatekeepers to the criminal legal system, is widely condemned by feminist researchers and advocates who see it as evidence of negligence and discriminatory attitudes about women.[32]

Societal beliefs about women who experience sexual violence also discourage women from reporting. Low reporting can partially be attributed to fear of being disbelieved.[33] According to a 2018 survey, only 5 percent of women who experienced sexual assault reported it to the police.[34] In comparison, 26 percent of women who were physically assaulted reported the assault.[35] In addition to the fear of not being believed, women reported fear of retaliation, shame and embarrassment, and a belief that the experience was minor and therefore not worthy of reporting.[36] Indigenous, Black, and racialized women commonly report revictimization by the police when they attempt to report violence.[37] A recent study of the experiences of Indigenous women in Canada who reported sexual violence to the police found that many Indigenous women felt the police had viciously denied their experiences of violence and made them feel as if they were being interrogated for committing a crime.[38]

Women's reluctance to formally report to the police is, ironically, another reason that they are vulnerable to defamation lawsuits. The threat of a civil lawsuit disproportionally impacts women who feel they do not have access to formal reporting mechanisms because of systemic marginalization, which may also deter them from seeking other remedies.[39] Toronto lawyer Lillian Cadieux-Shaw highlighted the fact that men who initiate defamation proceedings have something to gain whereas women who report "only face the prospect of harrowing litigation for their troubles." Furthermore, "when women find out that there is also the possibility that their perpetrator may bring retaliatory litigation against them ... why would any woman report?"[40]

The decision to delay reporting or to not report at all can become "evidence" in a defamation proceeding that the sexual violence did not occur and that the complainant must be lying. This happens even though it is well known that there are numerous barriers to reporting and a host of reasons why someone may choose to pursue another avenue to justice. Knowing that the legal system will likely fail them, women may seek informal justice.[41] Informal justice includes justice that is transformative or restorative and the use of social media.[42]

Some of the women I interviewed sought justice outside of the legal system by using alternative means of disclosing their experiences and seeking accountability from the person who caused harm. For example, some relied on informal communication after their formal report was dismissed or minimized by authorities; others were already aware of the realities of the legal system and made active choices to avoid becoming entangled in what they saw as an inherently flawed process. Whatever their reasons, their use of alternative routes to justice made them vulnerable to being sued. Indeed, this act of agency can be re-narrated in legal proceedings to shift the blame onto women: if sexual violence *actually* occurred, the argument goes, it would have been reported. But reporting to the police does not automatically offer legal protection from a defamation lawsuit. To date, this is an unexplored link in feminist legal and sociolegal critiques, one that bridges the civil and criminal legal systems' treatment of sexual violence and the vulnerability of those who experience sexual violence to the DARVO ethos in the legal system.

For antifeminist critics, the high rate of unfounded cases is proof that women frequently make false allegations. The systemic dismissal of reports of sexual assault alongside the deeply embedded myth that women frequently lie makes them especially vulnerable to being sued for defamation. Constance Backhouse expanded on the connection:

> Every time a woman speaks about sexual coercion or sexual assault, the cultural response is, "women lie." I would say 99.99 percent that is the initial reaction when a woman speaks. It's almost a 100 percent pushback that "women are lying, you're lying, women and children who speak about this lie." Consequently, we have a culture that is at odds with reality ... If you latch the ease of bringing a defamation action onto a culture that believes all women lie – they have the wind at their back. Any woman who makes those comments about a man can be labelled a liar, and a defamation suit can become just automatic. A defamation suit is the knee-jerk reaction within a culture that does not believe women.

Despite decades of feminist intervention and plenty of evidence to suggest otherwise, there is a deeply entrenched belief that false allegations of sexual violence are a common occurrence.

Breaking the Silence and Silencing Suits

When someone is accused of defamation, the first thing most lawyers will advise is that they refrain from repeating the allegedly defamatory statements and refrain from speaking about the legal proceedings until they are concluded, a process that can take years. Lawsuits have a widespread silencing effect. The lawsuit has the power to silence those who are sued, but it also instills fear in others that, if they speak out, they will be added to the lawsuit. Even the threat of a lawsuit can remove allegations of sexual violence from the public and private domain. It chills speech at an individual level (deterring those who have experienced sexual violence from speaking up) and a systemic level (silencing media reports and public discourse on allegations and sexual violence more generally).

For this reason, I argue that these lawsuits must be regarded as SLAPPs. SLAPPs are not necessarily initiated to test a case at trial but, rather, to entangle the defendant in a long and expensive legal process while simultaneously keeping them and others quiet about the issue.[43] At face value, these lawsuits look like ordinary civil claims, including defamation, malicious prosecution, abuse of process, conspiracy, and business torts. I argue that such lawsuits also chill public discourse about sexual violence.

Combine this chilling effect with fear of reporting and we are at risk of witnessing the disappearance of reports, disclosures, and discourse of sexual violence. This chilling effect will disproportionately harm women (who are statistically more likely to experience sexual violence) while protecting men (who are more likely to be perpetrators of sexual violence).[44] Ultimately, redressing sexual violence must outweigh the private reputational interests of men accused of sexual violence.

Discussions about sexual violence always, in one way or another, reference silence: why women remain silent about sexual violence; the ways women are systemically silenced (for example, the police denying or minimizing reports of sexual violence); or the tactics abusive men use to ensure that their victims remain silent. Debra Delaet and Elizabeth Mills noted that "a pattern of personal and political silence in response to sexual violence is evident in diverse societies across the globe. Silence shapes the reactions of survivors as well as the institutional responses of state and non-state actors."[45] Indeed, more generally, silence has long been considered a feature of femininity, "a trope for oppression, passivity, emptiness, stupidity or obedience."[46] Speaking about sexual violence challenges existing oppressive power structures.

Breaking the silence on sexual violence has become a central tactic of feminist resistance because silencing is the "universal tactic of perpetrators, imposed on victims of this crime unlike any other."[47] bell hooks stresses the importance of breaking the silence:

> Moving from silence into speech is for the oppressed, the colonized, the exploited, and those who stand and struggle side-by-side, a gesture of defiance that heals, that makes new life and new growth possible. It is that act of speech, of "talking back," that is no mere gesture of empty words, that is the expression of our movement from object to subject – the liberated voice.[48]

The #MeToo movement reignited the demand to break the silence on sexual violence. Following the viral hashtag, public discussion about sexual violence occurred on a global scale, largely attributed to social media, and became impossible to ignore. Shortly after, *Time* magazine named the Silence Breakers – from well-known movie stars and community organizers to hotel workers and office staff – the 2017 "Person of the Year."[49] This issue marked the historic significance of the #MeToo movement, noting the sheer volume of disclosures and the numerous political and legal actions being initiated internationally. The issue also recognized the intertwining of silence with sexual violence, which work together to disempower those who experience violence while protecting the perpetrators. Edward Felsenthal, editor-in-chief, said he chose the Silence Breakers as person of the year because of the incredible significance of "giving voice to open secrets, for moving whisper networks onto social networks, for pushing us all to stop accepting the unacceptable."[50] But as sexual violence discourse entered the public realm to an unprecedented degree, powerful men looked for ways to silence and push the allegations out of the public sphere and into obscurity. I argue that if such lawsuits continue, we will witness the disappearance of sexual violence discourse, not just in the public sphere but also in the private sphere.

Overview

This book guides readers through the experience of being sued with a defamation lawsuit. Chapter 1 offers a brief sociological introduction to civil law and procedure, highlighting my research participants' interpretations of each step. Chapter 2 critically examines the gendered underpinnings of defamation law and why it is such a useful tool for abusive men. Chapter 3 examines the range of consequences and the cost of being sued or threatened with a lawsuit. Chapter 4 examines the unique context of campus sexual violence. Chapter 5 puts evidence of the broad harms of retaliatory lawsuits into conversation with the literature on SLAPPs. In the conclusion, I recap the central arguments and offer recommendations to better protect silence breakers from retaliatory lawsuits.

A Note on Methods and Language
This research was conducted between 2019 and 2022. The research included semi-structured interviews; a review of policy, case law, and media articles; and an ethnography of two defamation proceedings (eight days observing in court). Of the participants, seventeen were sued or threatened with a lawsuit: six were threatened, nine were served, and two had lawsuits against them announced in the media but were never formally served. The research participants are not a homogenous group. They lived across Canada and occupied diverse social locations. The majority were cis women, and all but one were Canadian citizens. The one individual who was not a Canadian citizen and did not reside in Canada was included because the lawsuit against her was filed in Canada.

I also interviewed fourteen lawyers and antiviolence advocates who engaged in advocacy for silence breakers facing or threatened with legal action.[51] Again, the lawyers and antiviolence advocates represented a diverse sample from across Canada and worked in a range of settings, including large private-practice firms, sole practices, and not-for-profit organizations.

It is important to distinguish between reporting and disclosing sexual violence, the twin processes through which individuals communicate their experiences of sexual violence.[52] "Reporting" refers to those who register or attempt to initiate a formal complaint process either through the police or through other reporting mechanisms such as a professional regulatory body, the workplace, or a postsecondary institution. If, however, the individual decides not to issue a formal complaint but turns instead to their own forms of communication – such as social media, telling a trusted friend or family member about what happened, or seeking support services such as counselling – I refer to their actions as "disclosing" sexual violence.

I use the term "silence breaker" to refer to a range of individuals entangled within the civil law system, including not only those who are sued for reporting or disclosing sexual violence but also those who are sued for acting as bystanders responding to abusive behaviour they had witnessed or for supporting someone who disclosed or reported sexual violence. Thus, what these participants share is not necessarily an experience of sexual violence but their decision to come forward with what they know or witnessed, either to a variety of public authorities (such as employers, postsecondary institutions, or police) or via publicly accessible platforms such as social media or traditional media. "Silence breaker," therefore, is an accurate and encompassing term to describe the group of people whose experiences are discussed here.

My use of the term "sexual violence" intentionally relies on the World Health Organization's definition: "Any sexual act, attempt to obtain a sexual act, any unwanted sexual comments or advances, or acts to traffic, or otherwise directed, against a person's sexuality using coercion, by any person regardless of their relationship to the victim in any setting, including but not limited to the home and work."[53] I use the term "sexual violence" because it is broader and encompasses a wider range of behaviours, as opposed to terms such as "sexual assault" or "sexual harassment," which are legal terms with specific meanings.

Sexual violence is rooted in hegemonic notions about masculinity and femininity.[54] It is crucial to note the gendered underpinnings of sexual violence because the majority of adult sexual violence is perpetrated by cis men against women.[55] With that being said, this is not always the case, and it is crucial to acknowledge that women can be perpetrators of sexual violence, and men can be victims, facts that have been marginalized within sexual violence activism and scholarship.[56] This is not to suggest that gender is the only or even the dominant dimension of sexual violence; it is also reproduced through numerous mechanisms of structural oppression such as homophobia, racialization, ableism, and colonialism. Given that this is an exploratory study, and given the need to protect silence breakers from being identified in the findings, a major limitation of the research presented here is that I have been unable to clearly operationalize *how* intersecting modes of oppression allowed silence breakers to be targeted by perpetrators or the specific ways intersecting manifestations of structural oppression shaped the subsequent civil legal action. For example, three of the interview respondents noted that racism was a contributing factor in the legal action against them. While I would have liked to write about this, I couldn't include the blatant institutional racism they experienced and protect their identities because the specific context in which the allegations arose was widely reported in the media. Since lawsuits of this kind are still relatively rare, identifying even just a few minor details can "out" a research participant.

Finally, I do not use the term "criminal justice system"; instead, I use the term "criminal legal system." This usage challenges the notion that justice can be achieved within a system composed of patriarchal and colonial laws. In sexual violence cases, justice is rarely found within the confines of the law.[57]

1

A Civil Law Primer

Civil law and procedure are notoriously complex. In Canada, each province has its own rules of civil procedure, but in most substantive respects, they are similar.[1] This chapter provides a comprehensive overview of each step involved in a civil proceeding from a feminist sociological perspective. As research participants discussed the challenges associated with each step, they revealed how power dynamics can shape the civil legal process in sexual violence cases. An ostensibly objective system with the stated purpose of uncovering the truth can be used to position the plaintiff as the true "victim" of false allegations of sexual violence.

Cease and Desist

It's an undisputed fact that retaining a lawyer in Canada is expensive. For most Canadians, initiating a lawsuit is not financially viable, especially in cases where there isn't likely to be a large financial settlement. Even if there is a large settlement, the plaintiff may not be able to enforce the judgment if the defendant has no assets.[2]

It's more affordable to retain a lawyer to send a cease-and-desist letter to a silence breaker with the hope that the threat of a potential lawsuit will be enough to silence them. The cease-and-desist letter alerts the silence breaker that their actions are being monitored by the man accused of sexual violence and that legal action will be pursued if the activities persist. Three of the research participants received a cease-and-desist letter demanding a range of actions, including making no further statements about the violence, removing social media posts, and issuing a public apology along with a retraction of the claim. The letter often states that if the silence breaker does not comply with the request(s), legal action will be pursued. In most cases, the letter is nothing more than a threat, especially among men without the necessary financial resources. None of the men in these three cases followed through by filing a lawsuit.

Morgan's experience was emblematic. Morgan was in a long-term relationship with a man who routinely sexually, physically, and emotionally abused them. They were both part of an activist subculture that was explicitly antipolice. In an attempt to seek accountability from him, Morgan sought justice outside of the legal system by warning others in their community about his pattern of violent behaviour. Morgan told friends what happened in the relationship and wrote a vague post on social media outlining their experience of being abused. Shortly after posting, late one Friday afternoon, Morgan received an email from a lawyer representing their abusive former partner.

The subject line of the email read "[Ex-partner's name] v. [Morgan]," which Morgan described as intimidating "right off the bat." The letter alleged that Morgan had contacted their abuser's employer, resulting in him losing his job. Morgan was adamant that they never did this, yet the lawyer demanded that Morgan be held accountable. The demand letter requested that Morgan provide their former partner with a written apology and abstain from making similar statements in the future. If Morgan emailed this to their partner's former employer and took responsibility for the "misinformation," the employer would have no objection to him being rehired. The letter requested Morgan comply by noon on Monday or legal proceedings would be initiated for the damages, including his loss of employment. In addition to the overall – and deliberate – intimidating tone of this letter, it is notable that it was also sent late on a Friday afternoon. The lawyer requested that Morgan comply by Monday. This gave Morgan limited time to decide what action to take or to seek out legal advice.

Morgan googled the lawyer and learned they were a well-regarded senior lawyer at a large Toronto law firm:

> After a bit more googling, I realized [his lawyer] is on the same sports team as [former partner]. So, he's literally, like, just this hockey bro who happens to be a lawyer. So, he was like, "Hey man, can I buy you a beer

to write this letter to my bitch ex?" And to him, it's nothing, right? He's like, "Yeah, I would love to help intimidate your abused ex-girlfriend."

Morgan did not have the resources to defend themselves in a lawsuit, and their former partner was aware of this. Morgan understood his actions not only as a form of intimidation but also as a product of a particular kind of "bro culture" intended to bully Morgan into silence.

Luckily, like their ex-partner, Morgan could call upon their social network to respond to the legal threat. Morgan was employed in a job that provided services to several law firms. Morgan asked one of the lawyers with whom they had developed a working relationship about how to respond and assess the risk of their former partner following through with a lawsuit. The lawyer volunteered to write a response indicating Morgan would not comply with his demands. After the letter was sent, Morgan never heard from their former partner again:

> You know, getting his hockey buddy to send this email, just cost him a beer, and whatever. But at the same time, he probably was, "I'll write this email for you, but just letting you know, if they come back and they want to drop their gloves, you're going to have to pay me." So, it's either [former partner] changes to a shitty affordable lawyer, or [he] just gives up. And I'm guessing he knew that. I think he relied and wagered too heavily on his intimidation.

Although he never followed through, Morgan still felt that the threat of legal action was an abusive control tactic. The letter "fucks with your head. It's still controlling me from afar and dominating me from afar and like ... they just ... abusers will do whatever they can to not relinquish their control of the situation and their control of how people see them."

Although silence breakers can resist legal threats, as Morgan did, they are still impacted by the threat. A major challenge for silence breakers who receive such a letter is assessing the likelihood that whoever sent it will proceed to the next step: filing the lawsuit with the courts.

Commencing Legal Proceedings

Legal action officially begins with a written statement of claim. In Ontario, civil legal proceedings must be commenced within two years of the defamatory statement being made or published.[3] In Ontario, there are three levels of court for the hearing of such cases, and the amount the plaintiff is seeking determines which rules apply: small claims court (for claims up to $25,000), simplified procedure (for claims up to $100,000), and ordinary rules (for claims over $100,000). Regardless of the monetary amount of the claim, the plaintiff must issue a statement of claim with the court. Once the lawsuit has been issued, the plaintiff must serve the defendant(s) with the claim within six months unless the plaintiff has obtained a court order directing otherwise.[4] A statement of claim must be served personally (in person) on the defendant, unless the defendant agrees to "admit" service in some other form (such as responding to an email accepting service of the claim by email) or unless the court orders otherwise. Sometimes a copy of the claim will be left with another adult in the defendant's home or work.

Being served with a written notice of claim can come as a shock to defendants and, even if the case proceeds no further, exact a significant toll. For example, Catherine, a woman of colour who resides in a major Canadian city, noted that being served with a lawsuit by a man who had sexually violated her left her feeling isolated and without support:

> I was served at my work, but I wasn't at work that day. My coworkers had notified me that someone had come and was trying to serve me documents. I had this civil suit against me, and I didn't really know what to do. I told my mom, who did not react positively and was, unfortunately, very unsupportive. So, I was sort of on my own to find help to just navigate this.

Catherine and another person she knew were being sued by a man who had agreed to a peace bond with another woman following similar sexual violence allegations.[5]

Catherine, the plaintiff, the other defendant, and the woman that had the peace bond were members of a small community. It later became apparent that multiple men in the community were routinely sexually violating the women and gender-nonconforming people. Once the peace bond was made public, Catherine realized that he had victimized multiple people. To protect future victims, Catherine posted about the peace bond along with a summary of the sexual violence she had experienced:

> When I made those posts [on social media], it was at a time when my close friends and I and a bunch of other, like, nonmen were leaving this community and coming to realize that we had been serially abused and assaulted by these people that had authority over us. We knew that speaking about it would possibly blow back on us. We had been threatened with legal action. I remember at the time that I made those posts, that people were sharing them all over Facebook. I have screenshots of him saying, "Are there any lawyers out there who want to make a quick buck? Because I'm going to sue these people." But I think I was also pretty … like [I] was, like, twenty-three or twenty-four. These guys are wrong. What they did was wrong, and I think they know that. So, I felt like I knew it was risky, but I also had no idea what this was opening me up to.

While Catherine was aware that she might face legal action for the posts, she told me that she was naive about how the legal system works.

She came into the legal process expecting the courts to recognize the lawsuit as a retaliatory attack on her and others in the community. She was devastated when confronted by the reality of the legal response:

> When the judge was going to review the suit and set a date for the trial, and stuff like that, and give us a chance to mediate, I thought that the judge would look at what I had and throw it out. I was so convinced of my innocence and the fact that I was warning other people for their safety, and I had evidence of this person is doing unsafe things. Like, he was a drug dealer. He was having lots of parties where people were intoxicated and having sex. I put forward so much evidence about that. I had so many witnesses that could talk to this, speak on that. When I first entered that room and [the judge] just matter of fact looked over it and said, "Well you made these statements and you're going to have to defend that in court," I just completely broke down. And that's when I realized the reality of that system and the world that I am existing in at that point is not one where my innocence is assumed as well. It just seemed so absurd

to me that I lived in a world that if someone just had the money to get a lawyer, they could just sue me for whatever and drag me up and down the courts until I gave up.

Other participants did not take the lawsuit seriously when they first received the claim. Ali, a university professor, received a similar letter after he publicly supported several students in his department who had disclosed a range of abusive behaviours by a colleague, including unwanted sexual attention, sexual harassment, manipulation, and sexual coercion. Ali was initially bemused, if not amused, by the idea of a lawsuit:

> When I was first served with the notice of the lawsuit, my initial response was a great deal of laughter and disbelief at the ludicrous manner in which it was framed ... I was preparing to leave my [city] home to go to my parents in [city] for [a holiday]. I had switched off all of the lights, and checking my email on my phone, I read the notice in amazement. Because the house was empty, I allowed myself to laugh loudly. Thinking back, my laughter was in part because I knew that it was a completely flimsy case.

While it was, indeed, a flimsy case (the plaintiff would eventually abandon the lawsuit), Ali still needed to retain legal counsel to take the necessary steps to defend himself. Despite his belief that the case lacked legal merit, Ali noted that being served with the notice of claim ultimately caused him significant financial and emotional stress.[6]

Several options, or a combination of them, are available to the defendant once they have been served: file a statement of defence; file a notice of intent to defend followed by a statement of defence within ten days; try to settle all or part of the claim with the person suing them; counterclaim against the person suing; cross-claim against another defendant in the action; or start a third-party claim against someone who is not a party to the action.[7] If the defendant chooses to respond and lives in Ontario, the defence must be filed within twenty days of being served; if they live outside the province, they must file within forty days.[8] If the defendant does not file a defence, the plaintiff can request a default judgment from the court.[9] If the defendant has been noted in default because they have not responded to the claim, they are deemed to have admitted the truth of all allegations of fact made in the statement of claim and cannot take any further steps in the action. If noted in default, the defendant is also no longer entitled to notice of any steps in the action and will not be served with any further documents unless the courts rule otherwise.[10]

It's impossible to determine the outcome of lawsuits in Canada since the statistics collected on civil cases are limited each year to the number of cases initiated, the number of active cases, and the number of dispositions.[11] There is no information on cases that are settled after the statement of claim or those that simply do not progress within the legal system. The absence of quantitative data makes qualitative interviews more important. As the few examples cited here demonstrate, the act of serving someone with a lawsuit is often perceived by the defendant as a form of intimidation, humiliation, and retaliation.

Retaining Legal Counsel

Every silence breaker served with legal action sought legal information or legal advice.[12] Among them, the experience of retaining legal counsel differed substantially, most often because of social location or, in some cases, pure luck. Some sought legal information on defamation law online before posting about their experience with sexual violence on social media or making a formal report to authorities. Others sought legal advice by speaking to a lawyer prior to making sexual violence allegations.

These steps were taken to better prepare for any possible legal action taken against them. One research participant contacted a law professor at their university who specializes in defamation law under the guise that she planned to write a fictional story about defamation. Other research participants, like Morgan, Ali, and Catherine, did not seek legal advice until after the plaintiff initiated the action.

For some research participants, retaining legal counsel was a challenging experience; others had a much easier time. Research shows that having social ties – sometimes referred to as "contact resources" – is a form of social capital and may result in informal access to legal advice, information, or assistance.[13] As demonstrated in Morgan's case, participants with access to contact resources navigated the initial legal threat by having access to expert informants who could, at the very least, explain the processes and legal implications involved or help them initiate a response to the legal threat or claim.

Many of the silence breakers relied on lawyers in their social networks to assist them in different ways. For example, one silence breaker was close friends with a lawyer who agreed to represent her pro bono; another silence breaker worked as a process server and asked one of the lawyers they had developed a relationship with to assist them in responding to a cease-and-desist letter. Two of the silence breakers had law degrees and connections with the legal community. One participant, a professor, had a professional relationship through her university with a law professor who helped her draft her legal documents.

In contrast, participants with less social capital found the initial legal threat much more intimidating. Catherine, a young, racialized woman, received pro bono representation by pure chance. After being served, she went to a local not-for-profit legal help clinic to seek information about filing a defence. The volunteer lawyer assigned to help was struck by the case and called her a few days later, offering to represent her without pay:

> The lawyer who I had met with called me, and he says, "You know, I normally only volunteer once a year, but your case really stuck with me." So, he decided to take my case on pro bono, which was so amazing, so fortunate, because I can't imagine what I would have done if I didn't have his help and the help of his associates. They handled most of the paperwork. They went to all the settlement hearings with me. Any mediation, they were always there giving me advice and letting me know what I could do without any cost to me.

The compassion and diligence shown by Catherine's legal clinic lawyers are not the norm. More usually, not-for-profit organizations and free legal clinics can only provide minimal, if any, support. I interviewed two lawyers who work in not-for-profit legal clinics. Both told me that publicly funded legal clinics lack the expertise and resources to provide legal representation for complex defamation lawsuits against silence breakers. Shila, a lawyer working for a legal clinic that provides services to women who have experienced violence, added:

> Even for a two-day trial, the kind of resources that are needed, we do not have those at our disposal readily available. We have to pull out of frontline triage work when we take on a trial. As litigators, we want to do it. As lawyers, we would love to do more representation. We are choosing between helping five women with what to do in their situation and support them and handle it, or just take one client and work on her file and provide her representation. You have to choose your battles.

Lack of access to legal counsel was a common experience for some participants. For example, Elizabeth was an undergraduate student and single parent who had recently left an abusive marriage. She started an undergraduate degree to improve her financial situation. She had to see one of her professors in his office to speak to him about her accommodation needs for the class. After this appointment, the professor sexually assaulted her. She reported the sexual assault to the police and the university. The police did not lay charges, but the university fired the professor following her report. He then sued her, along with the university, for defamation.

Elizabeth did not have a social network to help connect her with a lawyer. Instead, she had to search for a lawyer on her own in the small Canadian city where she resided, a city where there were few lawyers with expertise in defamation law. Elizabeth contacted several lawyers. None would take her case. Reflecting on this experience, she explained, "Lawyers look at you and go, 'Unless you've got a hundred grand in the bank, I'm not going to talk to you.' Especially with a defamation lawsuit." Defamation lawsuits are notoriously complex and time-consuming, and even if Elizabeth won, there's no guarantee her legal bills would be covered.[14] This resulted in frustration and desperation: "First, I wanted somebody skilled, and then I got to a point where I was like, I just need a damn lawyer. I don't care if they're skilled ... It was whoever was willing to take my case." Elizabeth ended up retaining a junior lawyer who didn't have the professional expertise she was hoping for but was willing to represent her.

Many of the private bar lawyers I interviewed acknowledged the challenges involved in retaining legal counsel. Some talked about factors they consider before deciding whether to take a case. Of those who specialize in sexual abuse litigation, many are personal-injury lawyers who primarily work on contingency, meaning they will only take a case if they can recoup costs by countersuing for the sexual violence. There must be significant damages or an institution involved. One lawyer told me, "I've done a number of adult sexual assault cases as well, one or two or three, or whatever, but, yeah, I don't do a groping case just because it is not financially viable." Another lawyer explained why an institution needs to be involved:

> I take, maybe, one out of ten, in terms of the number of people who call me. I'm just not going to lead somebody down a garden path and in two years turn around and say, "Oh well, I'm not doing this anymore because it's a terrible case." And I'm not taking money from people. I will only work on a contingency basis. Because if it's not a good investment for my firm, it's not a good investment for some person who has a lot less financial resources than my firm does.

These lawyers confirm the challenges that Elizabeth and many others like her face when attempting to retain legal counsel to represent them in a defamation suit.

Overall, social capital and resource contacts significantly impacted the silence breaker's ability to retain legal counsel. Those who had a social connection with a lawyer were far more likely to have legal representation, even if the case would not be financially lucrative for the lawyer. Nonetheless, this does not mean that those with social capital retained legal counsel with ease. For many of the research participants, even those with full-time jobs, the financial burden of the lawsuit caused economic hardship, and they struggled to pay their legal bills.

Discovery

After written pleadings, the next stage of the legal process is discovery. Discovery is described as a time for legal counsel to assess the strength of the witnesses and the overall likelihood of success at trial.[15] Discovery has two phases: document exchange and oral discovery.[16] In most common law countries, parties only need to disclose the documents requested from opposing parties or "documents on which the party intends to rely."[17] The discovery rules in Canada are unique in comparison to other common law legal systems because they "provide for broad unilateral disclosure of documents."[18] Rule 30.02 states, "Every document relevant to any matter in issue in an action that is or has been in the possession, control or power of a party to the action shall be disclosed ... whether or not privilege is claimed in respect of the document."[19] A document can include a wide range of materials, including recordings, videotape, film, photographs, charts, graphs, maps, plans, surveys, accounts, and electronic data.[20]

Each party must produce three schedules of documents: documents the party has in their possession and do not object to producing; documents over which the party claims privilege (for example, communications with legal counsel); and documents that are no longer in the party's possession, control, or power (with an explanation and their location).[21] Each party is required to sign an affidavit affirming that the list of documents they previously had or currently have in their possession is accurate.[22] Each party must then provide the other party with the nonprivileged documents.[23]

The shift from "trial by ambush" to "trial by avalanche" means that the discovery process can become a war of attrition in which those with the greatest resources stand the greatest chance of victory. There may be benefits to a broad scope of discovery, but there are also consequences – for both parties. The British Columbia Justice Review Task Force noted that the sheer quantity of documents required has increased significantly over the past several years, contributing to increasing costs and delays for all parties:

> Many lawyers have commented that while discovery tools have successfully eliminated trial by ambush, they have replaced it with something that may be as bad or worse – trial by avalanche. We compared approaching the discovery stage of litigation to standing on the edge of a dark abyss. As litigants move forward they are required to descend into the abyss, and only the wealthiest are able to crawl up and out the other side.[24]

If either party is not satisfied with the documents provided, they can request further disclosure or information. If the opposing party is not forthcoming, a party may also bring forth a motion asking the court to require this information.[25] If documents pertaining to the legal case are lost or destroyed, a court may draw an adverse inference that the party was trying to hide information which could result in a finding of contempt of court.[26] The range of documents disclosed in this phase is often far broader than what will be provided to the court at trial.[27] Beyond worries of a document avalanche, there are unique concerns relating to document disclosure in cases that deal with allegations of sexual violence.

In these cases, discovery is unique in comparison to other types of civil cases, such as a business dispute or a claim against a media outlet. In a lawsuit against a silence breaker, the documents and records requested by the plaintiff often include intimate and personal details about the defendant's life. While it may be necessary to "prove his case," and to some extent is reasonable, the broad scope of the discovery process also gives the plaintiff intimate access to the defendant's private life, to the point of erasing their autonomy.

From the perspective of the law, the two parties are opponents on a level playing field with equal access to resources. To prove her case to the satisfaction of the court, the defendant is required to give up significant details about her private life. This is particularly true if she decides to counterclaim for the sexual violence. One lawyer explained the potential consequences:

> There are downsides to the civil suit. I guess the big one is that you have to open up your life to the [plaintiff] because of the fact that the law is quantifying the harm between what your life was and what it is now. You have to put yourself through the medical records, tax records, and education records, and that kind of stuff, and that is a difficult thing to do to someone that has already violated your trust and person.

As this lawyer notes, there is a fundamental imbalance of power in this process. The avalanche of private records and consequent intrusions on privacy can be particularly disturbing considering the abusive relationship that already exists between parties in a sexual violence suit. Even if the silence breaker decides not to countersue for damages relating to the sexual violence, she will likely still be required to provide records such as personal emails and text messages.

Researchers have spent little time examining the psychological or emotional impact of discovery in civil law, but parallels can be found in third-party and sexual-history requests in criminal sexual assault trials, which feminist academics have understandably focused on, and in document production in family violence law cases.[28] This work demonstrates the deeply invasive nature of such requests. While the expectation of privacy differs in family, civil, and criminal courts, the literature demonstrates that when a man with a history of violence seeks personal information about a silence breaker, the process itself contributes to the complex harms inherent in the sexual assault and subsequent legal processes. Private documents are used to render the woman who reported or disclosed sexual violence "crazy and unstable, prone to fabrication and unable to distinguish between reality and fantasy."[29] Over a decade ago, Lise Gotell cautioned that record requests in criminal legal trials could potentially result in the reprivatizing of sexual violence:

> If feminists broke the silence around sexualized violence in the last part of the twentieth century, we could say that ... the current period is one where a new silence is being re-established. Underlying the probing of complainants' sexual histories and records is the message that we need to be very careful about what we say about sexual assault. Discourses about sexual violence, once breaking into public discourse, are increasingly being re-privatized.[30]

I raise similar concerns about discovery in a civil lawsuit.

Even worse, silence breakers who have experienced sexual violence and find themselves in the civil legal system do not have the same legal protections that they would have in a criminal trial. Although the plaintiff must also disclose his correspondence and records, the power imbalance between the two parties does not render this exchange of documents neutral. Discovery sends a strong warning to people who have experienced sexual violence that they must be careful about what they disclose and to whom, out of fear that their private communications can be used to humiliate and discredit them.

The Examination

The next step in discovery is the examination. This may be an oral examination or, more rarely, a written one, consisting of questions and answers from both the defendant and plaintiff and, potentially, any witnesses who may be called at trial.

Oral discovery can be used by plaintiffs to strategically humiliate and intimidate silence breakers. Law professor Constance Backhouse spoke about the potential for the discovery process to exacerbate abusive power dynamics:

> Since most of these [cases] never get to trial, the lawyers that like to litigate look at discovery as their best shot, then, because they can't go into trial and swashbuckle their way around the courtroom, and so they pour all their resources into discovery, all their sleuthing, insinuations, and innuendos, trying to trip you up, find inconsistencies, find something about your past, get access to your records.[31]

Weyman Lundquist and Frank F. Flagal flagged the concerns raised by Backhouse nearly forty years ago, noting that "many litigators do not always use discovery as a trial aid to focus the issues; rather they engage in discovery to wear down opponents, to confuse, to delay, to increase expense and, ultimately, to settle lawsuits."[32]

Shila, another lawyer I interviewed, spoke about the impact of these unsettling tactics in sexual violence cases:

> These are tough cases. Evidence, the way it happens in a civil proceeding, is very complex and complicated. It is not necessarily happening in the presence of a judge. It is arranged with the lawyers and the person who is recording the discovery process. It can be a gruelling cross-examination-style discovery process. Very tough questions can be asked without any rape shield provisions. It is a very difficult process because the things that can be said without the presence of a judge, and without rape shield provisions, it can be complicated and a disheartening experience.

As Shila's comments indicate, the private nature of civil suits means that silence breakers may be subjected to a re-enactment of the power dynamics inherent in abuse. Furthermore, those who have experienced violence will be forced to revisit the sexual violence they experienced through the retrieval of documents and the oral discovery.

For researchers, these are difficult dynamics to get at, as the processes are confidential, and there is limited information about what happens in discovery beyond lawyers' descriptions of the process. Unlike trial transcripts, oral examination transcripts are not available to the public, rendering them difficult to either analyze or regulate.

Fortunately, the exceptional case of Marilou McPhedran, who was sued by the Ontario Medical Association (OMA), provides some clues about what goes on in discovery.[33] In 1991, McPhedran, a human rights lawyer, chaired the Task Force on Sexual Abuse of Patients commissioned by the College of Physicians and Surgeons of Ontario after an exposé of the college's cases in the *Globe and Mail,* which led to major changes to Ontario law. In 2000, during a mandatory governmental review of that law, McPhedran was appointed by the Conservative minister of health, Elizabeth Witmer, to head another task force, this time to assess the impacts of the laws on patients who reported experiencing sexual exploitation by all regulated health professionals, not just physicians, and the subsequent institutional processes covered by the law.[34] In June 2001, McPhedran was the primary author of the final *Independent Report of the Special Task Force on Sexual Abuse of Patients by Regulated Health Professionals in Ontario.* McPhedran also published a one-thousand-word opinion piece in the *Globe and Mail* summarizing the findings of the task force with a specific focus on doctors who sexually abuse their patients.[35] In the article, McPhedran drew attention to a case where a doctor found guilty of professional misconduct for having sex with one of his patients had his licence revoked. The doctor appealed the revocation of his licence, and the OMA acted as an intervenor to argue that the revocation was a breach of his Charter rights. In her opinion piece, McPhedran argued that the OMA should not have intervened; it should have funnelled its resources into the prevention of sexual abuse by doctors. The OMA sued McPhedran for her opinion piece but elected not to sue the *Globe and Mail.*

The lines of questioning McPhedran had to endure in the discovery demonstrate a gendered nature. McPhedran was a highly regarded professor and lawyer, with a noted history of respected leadership in advocating against sexual violence. The OMA lawyer, Hansel J.B.A. Dickie, QC, started the oral discovery by asking to see her curriculum vitae but then shifted to asking about her marital status. Later in the oral examination, Dickie returned to inquiring about the marital status of the other experts appointed to the task force:

> *Dickie:* These experts on sexual abuse, I don't know how to put it any better than this, but had they been out in the real world very much? Were they married?
>
> *MacLeod Rogers (counsel for McPhedran):* I don't think Ms. McPhedran needs to answer that question.
>
> *McPhedran:* I can't answer that question. I wasn't on a personal basis.

Dickie sexualized McPhedran throughout the discovery process. Dickie put forward several hypothetical situations of sexual activity between doctor and patient and showed an inclination to place himself and McPhedran into each of the scenarios he posed about "acceptable" sexual conduct:

> *Dickie:* Did the committee give consideration to circumstances such as this; you come in to see me and you say, I've got a cold, Dr. Dickie, for I am now a doctor. I've got a cold, Dr. Dickie. Can you give me something for it, and I do, whatever doctors give out for colds, and as you walk out the door, Ms. McPhedran, I sweep you into my arms and I give you a great smack on the mouth and I run my hands down your body and you go out and say oh, my. I take it that I have committed sexual abuse.
>
> *McPhedran:* Yes.
>
> *Dickie:* I go home that night and I'm subject to mandatory revocation of my license, no doubt, if prosecuted properly.
>
> *McPhedran:* If prosecuted.
>
> *Dickie:* Okay. I go home that night and there you are, cooking dinner, and it just so happens you and I are married, Ms. McPhedran. Does the committee still intend that I should lose my licence for kissing my wife in my office?
>
> *McPhedran:* Well, there is a fair bit of attention paid to that sort of scenario, Mr. Dickie.
>
> *Dickie:* Could you just answer the question, madam?

This line of questioning was not isolated. It proceeded throughout the oral discovery:

> DICKIE: Well, characterize then someone who came to the doctor and decided to have a relationship with the doctor, sexual in nature, solely as a consequence of his licentious desires and not at all as a consequence of any transferal. Did you consider that?
>
> MCPHEDRAN: We didn't discuss it in those terms, Mr. Dickie.
>
> DICKIE: Thank you.
>
> MCPHEDRAN: Because none of the research or the expertise available to us indicated that is a likely scenario.
>
> DICKIE: What about a hub of common sense, just for somebody to put it as I did, nobody even put it like that?
>
> MCPHEDRAN: I wouldn't agree with you that's common sense. I would agree with you that that's – I would have to say ignorance.
>
> DICKIE: Ignorance. All right. Well, how about a whore?
>
> MCPHEDRAN: Could you define whore for me, please.
>
> DICKIE: Yes, a woman who sells –
>
> MCPHEDRAN: Do you mean a sex trade worker by that terminology?
>
> DICKIE: A woman who sells sex.
>
> MCPHEDRAN: A woman only?
>
> DICKIE: Or a man who sells sex. I was speaking in this instance of a woman because in comes. Example – or we can reverse it if you'd like. In comes a woman to the doctor and the doctor treats her, and it's relatively minor. I don't know. She's got the flu that was going around a couple of months ago and sidelined everybody in a lot of law offices. She says, what do I take for the flu, doctor, and the doctor treats her and says come back next week, or at least in three or four days and she says, doctor, how about tonight? The doctor says what do you mean, and she says, "I'm a whore. I charge $100.00 an hour. See you at my place. Bring the C-Note." The doctor goes along that night. Is he abusing the woman now?

These exchanges are emblematic of the approach taken by the plaintiff throughout the oral-discovery process.

There were few questions directly related to the allegations of defamation. Instead, counsel for the OMA focused on interrogating McPhedran about her perspectives on sexual activity between doctor and patient and, generally, sexualizing the interrogation process itself. In my interview with McPhedran, she told me that during the recess she saw the female court reporter in the washroom. The reporter expressed how upset she was hearing the lines of questioning McPhedran was subjected to by the OMA lawyer. McPhedran's own lawyer also called a recess during the cross-examination because of the inappropriate lines of questioning. McPhedran asked that her lawyer not object to any of the questions posed by the OMA lawyer. She wanted his conduct recorded for the judge to see if the case proceeded to trial.

The discovery transcript reveals the discriminatory lines of questioning silence breakers are often subjected to in cross-examination. Shocking as the transcript is, it is also worth noting that McPhedran was fortunate to enjoy several advantages relative to other participants in this study. As a lawyer by training, she had more knowledge about navigating the legal system than most of the research participants I spoke with (which may explain why she allowed Dickie to expose himself on the record). Perhaps more importantly, McPhedran was not involved in the case as a victim of sexual violence, and the lawsuit against her was initiated by an organization, not a man who victimized her.

As Shila noted, the discovery may be even more brutal for those being examined on their direct experiences of sexual violence. Indeed, many of the research participants described the civil legal process as resembling a criminal sexual assault trial. Laura, a silence breaker, described being questioned by the plaintiff's lawyer: "The lawyer pretty much aggressively cross-examined me about the assault and said it was consensual. You don't know what assault is. You're confused. Blah, blah, blah. Asked me a bunch of questions in front of the guy who did it." The entire legal process had a profound impact on Laura's emotional well-being: "I was pretty shaken up after that. I was really retraumatized by being forced into the meeting like that, with the perpetrator, like that, staring me down."

Laura found it particularly difficult because she was assaulted by her boss, and their employer helped to preserve his reputation once he initiated legal action:

> I was just really shaken up by these people that I worked with and trusted were, like, threatening me during a crisis. I just felt they just completely

lost their moral compass and have crossed lines ... I think that's what shook me up the most. I didn't know these people could be capable of that. Or, if they even knew how harmful it was, what they were doing.

Given the limited data, these findings cannot be generalized to make conclusions about the discovery process overall. The private nature of discovery makes it incredibly difficult to conduct meaningful research on what happens outside the courtroom. Interviews do show, however, that discriminatory stereotypes about people who experience sexual violence are present in the civil legal system. The discovery process can allow abusive men to legally gain access to private records, which can be a form of revictimization for those who have experienced sexual violence.

Mediation

There are financial motivations to settle before a trial. According to the 2021 Legal Fees Survey, preparing for a five-day civil trial in Canada (excluding the costs of the trial) costs $38,194.35 while a seven-day trial costs $92,118.[36] In 2019, the average national hourly rate for a civil litigation lawyer with two to five years of experience was $253.18.[37] Legal fees and disbursements prove to be a significant barrier to successfully defending a lawsuit. Several participants noted that if they had been able to financially, they would have taken their cases to trial: "I would have needed twenty or thirty grand to take that through a trial. I don't have that. If somebody is sexually assaulted and speaks out about it and gets sued, that's an enormous amount of financial burden. I feel there's a level of that. And why are lawyers making $500 an hour?"[38]

Money, however, is not the only barrier to going to court. Other participants felt a trial would contribute to their revictimization. Similarly, plaintiffs may wish to settle before trial to avoid the possibility of unflattering information circulating about the allegations.

The majority of the cases studied here did not proceed beyond mediation, either because the parties reached a mutual agreement or because the plaintiff withdrew the lawsuit. Although it may be assumed that having a case withdrawn would be a significant relief for someone being sued, many reported that they felt angry and frustrated because they wanted vindication from the court. According to Ali: "When I realized that the case against me would evaporate, I felt intensely angry, as some part of me wanted the case to go to court. I wanted to confront him and clear my name. I felt angry that I would not have the chance to see the look on his face as his case fell to pieces."

McPhedran expressed a similar sense of frustration. The day before the trial was set to begin, the OMA withdrew the lawsuit against her. She had been confident that her cause was just, but, as she recounts, her lawyers reminded her of the legal system's unpredictability:

> My lawyer had to take me outside and said to me, "We are not going with you on this. If you refuse this walking away, of course, we will represent you at trial, [but] we will not participate in an appeal." I said, "I don't think I am going to lose." They said, "You shouldn't lose. You are clearly in the right here, but strange things happen in the legal system all the time, and you need to know we are at the end of our line."

Although agreeing to walk away was heartbreaking, and McPhedran was distraught at the loss of an opportunity to vindicate herself and reveal what the OMA was hiding, she'd be bankrupt if she lost. McPhedran reflected on these potential costs: "My only hesitation about trial was that I couldn't afford it. I was a single mom with my firstborn asking me at the dinner table, 'Mom, are we going to lose the house?' And I had to say, 'Yes, honey, we are going to lose the house if I lose the case.'"

The Trial

There is a significant risk in going to trial, not just because of the cost of legal counsel but also because losing the case means possibly having to pay damages to and legal fees for the other party.[39] Further, there may be some details of the case that both parties would not want to be made public. Almost all civil cases in Canada are tried by a judge, who determines the case on a balance of probabilities.[40] If the defendant is found not liable, the judge will dismiss the case. If the defendant is found liable, however, a judge will consider the following before deciding what the damages will be: the remedy that the plaintiff has requested, the facts of the case, and compensation for the plaintiff.[41] In Canada, typically, the party who loses a civil proceeding or motion has to make a significant contribution to the winning party's costs.[42] Several factors are taken into consideration when making a judgment about costs, such as the amount recovered in the proceedings, the relative success of each party, the complexity of the proceeding, and the conduct of the parties during the legal process.[43] As mentioned, few civil cases make it to trial. Only two of the silence breakers I interviewed had cases that went to trial.

The Publication Ban

For some of the silence breakers, the lawsuit against them allowed the media, the plaintiff, and his supporters to name them either in traditional media outlets or on social media. For example, one woman made what she thought was a confidential report of sexual assault only to have her name and the details of the sexual assault published by a national media outlet after the accused decided to sue her for defamation. Her name remains linked to the case on the internet. In contrast, in a criminal sexual assault trial, sexual assault complainants are protected by a publication ban unless they opt to remove it, meaning that any information that could identify the complainant or a witness cannot be published or broadcast under section 486.4 of the Criminal Code. The publication ban remains in effect regardless of the outcome of the case.[44]

In the late 1980s, the publication ban was challenged as being unconstitutional because it violated the freedom of the press, as protected under section 2 of the Charter.[45] The Supreme Court of Canada upheld the legislation. In the decision, Justice Lamer stated that the legislation protects victims of sexual assault "from the trauma of widespread publication resulting in embarrassment and humiliation."[46] The Supreme Court justices reasoned that protecting the identities of those who report sexual assault would encourage reporting and, in turn, deter sexual violence in the future. While this decision, and the publication ban in general, has not eliminated the embarrassment and humiliation of testifying as a complainant in a sexual assault trial, the ban is likely preferable for some, perhaps many, sexual assault complainants since the publication of details relating to an alleged sexual assault may negatively impact the complainant's mental health, relationships, employment, safety, and privacy.[47]

In contrast, in civil proceedings, no similar protections are guaranteed, even if the lawsuit is a direct result of reporting or disclosing sexual violence. The absence of an automatic publication ban in civil law does not mean that a defendant cannot ask the court to issue one. In 2019, publication bans were sought to protect the defendants in *Galloway* and *Stuart v Doe*.

In both instances, the defendants were being sued for defamation after they reported faculty members to their respective postsecondary institutions for sexual assault.[48] In both cases, the courts granted the requested publication ban in favour of the privacy of the women.

There are striking similarities between the two cases. As a result of being reported for sexual assault to their employers, both men were subject to workplace investigations and, subsequently, lost their jobs. After the institutional investigations were completed, both women contributed to public dialogue about their experiences of sexual violence and reporting the violence to postsecondary institutions. In *Galloway*, A.B., a professional artist, was sued for a public art exhibition in New York City about the experience of reporting sexual violence to campus administrators. In *Stuart*, Jane Doe made a public Facebook post and a drawing commemorating the #MeToo movement but did not personally identify herself as a survivor of sexual assault or name the man who assaulted her.[49]

Neither the men accused nor the universities involved were named by A.B. or Jane Doe. In many ways, the two women did what "good victims" are expected to do – they made a formal report to their postsecondary institutions and remained silent until the investigations were completed. They engaged in public speech without specifically identifying the men or the postsecondary institutions involved. Yet they were still sued for defamation by men seeking to rehabilitate their professional reputations through legal means and, arguably, to punish the women who'd caused them reputational harm.

Since neither of the men consented to the defendants' requests for a publication ban, the women were required to make an argument to the court about the need to have their identities protected.[50] In both decisions, the courts noted the competing interest of open-court principles and the privacy of someone who has made a sexual assault allegation. In both cases, the courts found in favour of privacy and granted the publication bans. The motion judges' decision to grant the publication ban in both cases was attributed to the fact that although the lawsuit received public attention, the identities of the women were relatively unknown.[51] The court noted that A.B. was granted a publication ban because she'd been selective in who she disclosed the sexual violence to.[52] The court also noted that A.B.'s art exhibition "was about her experience as a survivor of sexual assault – she did not identify the plaintiff and the exhibit was not publicly linked to the plaintiff."[53] Here, the motion judge constructs the "good victim" as one who protects the identity of the accused and confines disclosures about the violence she experienced to those within her close social circle.

These decisions suggest that publication bans in civil trials are reserved for women who rely on the formal investigative process, regardless of how problematic, slow, or discriminatory it may be. Further, it seems that publication bans on proceedings are only available to women who can demonstrate that they are compliant and "good" victims.[54] There is an expectation that women will remain quiet to keep their identities – and the identities of the men they accuse – hidden. In the following chapter, I examine the linkage between the idealization of women's modesty and the history of defamation law. Here, suffice it to say that the courts have yet to recognize the significant difference between choosing to engage in the public sphere as a victim, which allows some agency over what details will be shared, and a civil trial, in which victims have little control over what details of their lives are entered into the public record.

Through an overview of the procedural and practical steps involved in a lawsuit, this chapter demonstrates the challenges in navigating the civil legal system from the perspectives of people who have been sued or threatened with a lawsuit. Civil procedure textbooks present the legal process as a straightforward process, but, as many of the silence breakers explained, this is often not the case. Unsurprising, legal textbooks, written from the perspective that the law is a neutral and objective arbiter, fail to account for how power dynamics between parties, such as disparities in terms of access to financial resources and legal representation, can shape legal proceedings, such as the documentary and oral-discovery processes. For almost all the silence breakers, the plaintiff was more privileged in terms of social location and access to financial resources. These disparities were particularly pronounced in the case of silence breakers who were queer, racialized, gender-diverse, or worked low-wage jobs without job security.

The silence breakers' narratives demonstrate how power dynamics between the plaintiff and defendant can be used strategically to advance legal action. Such power dynamics can be heightened depending on various factors that may influence her ability to defend herself, including her income, profession, and overall positionality as a "good victim," which is often entangled with discriminatory stereotypes intertwined with racism, colonialism, and ableism.

Abusive men can use the process to mimic abusive dynamics; they can intimidate and silence their victims and those who support them before a legal proceeding is initiated. The absence of the scaffolded protections for complainants available in criminal sexual assault trials – such as the automatic availability of publication bans and rules that limit the use of private records and questioning the victim about her sexual history – means that silence breakers are often subjected to private legal action that leaves them vulnerable to public humiliation, shaming, and revictimization. Overall, the presence of differential power dynamics between plaintiff and defendant and the calculated use of rape myths allow abusive men to strategically use the civil legal system to foster abusive power dynamics under the guise of "truth" seeking and the redemption of their tarnished reputations.

2

The Gender of Reputation

Reputation is considered so important that an entire body of law – defamation law – exists solely to protect people from reputational harm. In 1929, prominent English tort scholar Sir Frederick Pollock wrote that "reputation and honour are no less precious to good men than bodily safety and freedom. In some cases, they may be dearer than life itself."[1] Such sentiments remain intact, as demonstrated by recent legal decisions. To date, the Supreme Court of Canada's most in-depth explanation of the importance of reputation is in *Hill v Church of Scientology of Toronto*.[2] The Supreme Court of Canada defined "good reputation" as being "closely related to the innate worthiness and dignity of the individual."[3]

The importance placed on men's reputations is also present in criminal law. For example, Gillian Balfour tracked criminal cases in Manitoba where men were charged with violent offences, and found that criminal courts tend to treat male violence, especially when enacted by white men, as a reasonable and normal response to perceived threats to their reputation.[4] But even though the common law tradition stresses reputation as a fundamental quality of democratic society, there are few definitions of "good reputation."[5] Given that reputation is intangible, experienced through interpersonal relationships and intertwined with an individual's sense of worth, reputation is arguably a sociological concept rather than a legal one.[6] Defamation is also inherently social: for a statement to be actionable, it must be communicated to a third party, meaning that its very existence requires some form of social interaction.[7] This chapter examines defamation law as a legal construction and as a normalizing discourse of gender and reputation.

A Sociolegal Introduction to Defamation in Canada

By the sixteenth century, common law action for defamation had become commonplace.[8] The common law of defamation was created to reduce reliance on the duel "as a method for vindication of reputation," as it was "regarded by the monarchy as being particularly dangerous to the stability of the State."[9] The link between violence and defending male honour continues to characterize the law. In *Hill*, Justice Cory wrote: "Though the law of defamation no longer serves as a bulwark against the duel and blood feud, the protection of reputation remains of vital importance."[10] Despite the law's insistence that men should be able to protect their reputations, legal scholars since the early twentieth century have criticized the common law of defamation for being "old and out of date, moss covered with age," "absurd in theory and very often mischievous in its practical operation," and "infected with the foolish conceits, absurd paradoxes, superstition, and artificial reasoning of a semi-barbarous age."[11] Despite this long-standing criticism (along with shifting societal views about the importance of expression and speech and radical changes in communications technologies), the tort of defamation has changed little over the centuries.[12]

Under common law, there are two categories of defamation – slander and libel. "Slander" refers to oral communication while "libel" refers to written communication, and each constitutes a distinct category governed by different legal regimes.[13] In slander cases, the rules are tilted in favour of the defendants.[14] To succeed, the plaintiff must prove they suffered pecuniary damages: a quantifiable monetary amount must be attached to the damages cited for the claim to be actionable.[15] There are exceptions. A plaintiff can claim slander when seeking redress from words that (1) disparaged them in their trade or profession, (2) imputed the commission of a criminal offence, (3) imputed a "loathsome or contagious disease," or, in the case of women, (4) imputed their "unchastity."[16] The common law has a long-standing interest in preserving reputation.

In comparison to slander, the rules of libel tilt in favour of the plaintiff. Libel is a strict liability tort, meaning that the plaintiff does not have to prove there was negligence or an intention to cause harm.[17] The plaintiff only needs to demonstrate that the printed words refer to the plaintiff, could be read as defamatory, and have been published to at least one third party.[18] Under libel law, there is no burden for the plaintiff to demonstrate that the statement is untrue or that the defendant was at fault for publishing the allegedly defamatory words.[19] Further, to collect damages, the plaintiff does not have to demonstrate that they suffered a loss; the damage to their reputation is presumed.[20] Libel cases are far more common than slander cases in Canadian courts.[21]

The Preservation of Reputation

Legal scholar Jerome Skolnick writes that "defamation is a distinctively sociological tort" because at its core it is about the protection of an "individual's projection of self in a society."[22] Reputation is highly relational; it involves three relational acts: "An act of attribution in which someone attaches an (evaluative) quality to someone else; an act of sharing, in which this attribution is communicated to others; and an act of perception in which this attribution is recognized and understood by a receiver."[23] Reputation is also unique because while people have control over many aspects of their reputation, including their actions and other biographical information (for example, where they went to school or their professional designation), the reputational assessment is ultimately done by others.[24] Reputation cannot exist without another person, or a community, forming a judgment about an individual that in turn guides future interactions between said individual and others.[25] Reputation is not a tangible object but can have serious implications for many aspects of a person's life, ranging from economic opportunities to social networking and even romantic relationships.[26]

The ethereal attributes of reputation are given material effect through laws designed to mitigate against reputational harm. For example, in *Hill*, the Supreme Court of Canada extensively examined the importance of a "good reputation." Justice Cory, writing for the majority, wrote:

> To most people, their good reputation is to be cherished above all. A good reputation is closely related to the innate worthiness and dignity of the individual. It is an attribute that must, just as much as freedom of expression, be protected by society's laws. In order to undertake the balancing required by this case, something must be said about the value of reputation.[27]

Cory established that while reputation is not explicitly mentioned in the Charter, "the good reputation of the individual represents and reflects the innate dignity of the individual, a concept which underlies all the *Charter* rights. It follows that the protection of the good reputation of an individual is of fundamental importance to our democratic society."[28]

The Supreme Court of Canada continues to value the role of male reputation. In November 2019, Joanna Birenbaum, a Toronto lawyer specializing in sexual violence litigation, made submissions for the Barbra Schlifer Commemorative Clinic as an intervenor at the Supreme Court of Canada to urge the courts to protect women from retaliatory lawsuits. As Birenbaum began her submissions, Justice Rowe interrupted her to ask about men, whose reputations would be damaged by false allegations of sexual violence:

> BIRENBAUM: Justices, the Schlifer Clinic intervenes in this appeal because survivors of sexual violence across Canada should not have to think about whether or not they have the emotional and financial capacity to withstand a lawsuit before they report to the police, or their employer or their school, or before they reach out for help from trusted persons in their lives. Lawsuits against women who disclose sexual violence, they are not a hypothetical problem, they are not an anticipated problem …
> ROWE: What about if the allegation is 100 percent false? What happens to the person who is accused?
> BIRENBAUM: We need to take a step back. We do not have a social problem, systemic social crisis of false reports.
> ROWE: It's a problem for the person's reputation who is now destroyed.
> BIRENBAUM: … Disclosures of sexual violence ought to be given significant weight, because, your honours, the crisis of violence against women in this country can only be addressed, or at least in part, by individual women coming forward and disclosing and reporting. It is on the backs of individual women that this social crisis can be addressed …
> The overwhelming majority of disclosures of sexual violence are true.
> ROWE: What about the ones that aren't?

Despite Birenbaum's assurances that false accusations are rare, and her attempt to have the Supreme Court consider the social, public and, indeed, legal implications of silencing speech related to systemic gendered violence, Rowe's interruptions made it clear that, when it comes to sexual violence, his primary concern is the reputation of men falsely accused.

Inherent in Justice Cory's and Rowe's responses is the belief that reputation is a vitally important entity that can be easily endangered and must be protected. Reputation, however, is historically and socially contingent.[29] It's worth examining the history of reputation as it has been understood over time in law and in the academic literature. Robert Post has identified three ways reputation is conceptualized in the legal terrain: as property, as honour, and as dignity.[30] Post acknowledged that while these three are not the only possible conceptualizations of reputation, they had the "most important impact on the development of the common law of defamation."[31] Reputation as honour was the prevalent perspective in pre-Industrial England during the formative years of defamation law. "Reputation as honour" refers to the social position of the individual.[32] Today, however, the idea of honour has faded in favour of the concepts of "reputation as property" and "reputation as dignity."

In the concept of reputation as property, character is a form of capital; it "presupposes that individuals are connected through the institution of the market."[33] Reputation shares many characteristics with things we consider property; it has economic value that is derived from the market, and it is the basis for compensation.[34] For example, a lawyer with a good reputation can charge a higher fee than a lawyer with a poor professional reputation.[35] The ontological status of reputation as property is not created until it reaches the economic or intellectual marketplace.[36]

The fact that reputation cannot exist without the judgment of others marks a significant difference from other traditional forms of property, which are often tangible items.[37] In this conceptualization, the good name one builds for oneself is tied to one's ability to successfully navigate a competitive market. If another person undermines one's ability to compete in the market by carelessly or maliciously circulating false information about them, it becomes a legal harm. It follows that monetary compensation is an appropriate remedy for this kind of reputational damage. It is common for a plaintiff to cite economic consequences because of a loss of employment or job opportunities following allegations of sexual violence. For example, some plaintiffs evaluate their reputations as having experienced so much harm from the allegations of sexual violence that they seek millions of dollars in damages.[38] Post's conceptual category "reputation as property" helps us understand economic evaluations of reputation; however, not all reputational damage is instrumentally tied to the market.[39]

"Reputation as dignity" refers to the relationship between the public and private aspects of reputation.[40] Reputation as dignity differs from reputation as property because "dignity is not the result of individual achievement, and its value cannot be measured in the marketplace. It is instead 'essential' and intrinsic in 'every human being.'"[41] From this perspective, "the law of defamation can be conceived as a method by which society polices breaches of its rules of deference and demeanor thereby protecting the dignity of its members."[42] Therefore, defamation law has a dual function: protecting an individual's dignity and enforcing society's interest in maintaining civility. Cases that involve the loss of dignity are not necessarily about the monetary award, because dignity cannot be restored through money. Rather, if the court can establish that statements were untrue and defamatory, the individual's conception of their own self-worth may be restored and their exclusion from their community reversed.[43]

Reputation as dignity has been recognized by the Supreme Court of Canada. In *R v Lucas*, the court considered the appeal of Mr. and Mrs. Lucas, convicted of criminal defamation for picketing outside a police station. They'd held placards that specifically named a police officer, falsely accusing him of knowingly placing a child in danger of sexual abuse.[44] The Supreme Court agreed with the trial judge that the defendants "should have known that the statements on their placards were false"; the majority held that "the protection of an individual's reputation from willful and false attack recognizes both the innate dignity of the individual and the integral link between reputation and the fruitful participation of an individual in Canadian society."[45] As this case illustrates, and as Post confirms, defence of reputation is about more than restoring economic loss; it's also about restoring one's dignity.

Dignity is inherent to us all and clearly important, but it is fragile. Vagueness notwithstanding, the courts seem confident that they will recognize harm to dignity when they see it. As Justice Goodman stated in a civil defamation case involving a disclosure of childhood sexual abuse by two sisters to their family, "I agree with the plaintiff's final submission in that a good reputation is closely related to innate worthiness and dignity of the individual. False allegations can also very quickly and completely destroy a good reputation. A reputation tarnished by libel can seldom regain its former luster."[46] From Justice Goodman's viewpoint, the loss of a "good reputation" is closely linked to dignity, and the suitable remedy involves restoring "lustre" to a person who has been tarnished by defamation.

A defamation lawyer I interviewed, who had represented both plaintiffs and defendants, noted that, for some plaintiffs, the purpose of the lawsuit is not necessarily to seek monetary damages but rather vindication from the courts and the restoration of their reputations in the community: "Vindication ... sometimes ... really is the key motivation for plaintiffs in defamation matters because they want the piece of paper – a judge saying, 'This was defamatory' ... Often, it's not about the money at all." The time and money required to proceed with a lawsuit, along with the low likelihood of receiving a large monetary award, suggests that plaintiffs have nonmonetary motivations. For example, in *Whitfield v Whitfield*, Bryan Whitfield was only awarded $5,000 in damages.[47] His "win" signalled something else: vindication.

While Post's exploration of reputation helps tease out its various relational and legal qualities, it fails to take into consideration the gendered nature of defamation law. Post's work focuses on male reputation and its legal manifestations, even as he presents these conceptualizations as if they were universal. Women have historically used, and continue to use, defamation law for vastly different purposes than men, and the mobilization of reputation as either property or dignity does not apply so easily to women's defamation actions.[48] Women, unlike men, have most often attempted to protect their reputation from degrading comments about their sexuality. For this reason, Diane Borden has argued that women's experiences of defamation law do not fit into Post's typologies.[49] While the types of cases and courts' responses have shifted dramatically over time, women's defamation actions reveal that discriminatory societal assumptions about women's sexuality remain embedded within defamation law.

From the late nineteenth century to the early twentieth, when women did sue for defamation, it was usually for claims of sexual slander – verbal accusations that she'd engaged in behaviours such as adultery, sex work, premarital sex, or other activities deemed "sexually deviant."[50] Borden's study of US defamation cases in 1897–1906 and 1967–76, two periods marked by the women's rights movement and women entering the public sphere in greater numbers, found that women were plaintiffs in only 21.9 percent of slander cases. They were often successful, but the courts awarded them much lower amounts than men.[51] Between 1897 and 1906, male plaintiffs received damages amounting to more than double the damages awarded to women.[52] By the late 1960s and '70s, this disparity had increased: men were awarded more than eight times the average amount of damages awarded to women.[53] Women continued to be successful in actions relating to damages to their personal reputations, but they were unsuccessful in 80 percent of the actions brought forward for damages to their professional reputations.[54] Such findings demonstrate how the decisions in these cases reinforce stereotypes about women's virtue and domesticity.

Straightforward sexual slander cases alleging "unchastity" started to taper off in the 1960s. Defamation claims by women shifted to what Lisa Pruitt calls "new chastity," defined as an attempt, often by media outlets, to ridicule, degrade, and humiliate women in relation to their sexuality and "sexual personhood," often in the form of parody.[55] In the United States, for example, Kimberli Jayne Pring, former Miss Wyoming, initiated a lawsuit against a publication for running a sexually graphic parody story about her.[56] In another case, a woman sued a television show for using unauthorized videos of her juxtaposed with graphic sexual imagery.[57] Pruitt notes that both traditional chastity cases and new chastity cases reinforce women's association with the private sphere, specifically sexual propriety.[58] These cases differed from previous generations because the matter was not about a woman's chastity but rather her public degradation. Unlike in the past, where courts tended to take a paternalistic role to protect a woman's virtue, to ensure she was able to participate in the nuclear family, the new chastity cases are rarely successful. The courts are far more concerned about the preservation of free speech than women's reputations.[59]

In researching this book, I found only one study on the gendered implications of defamation law in Canada.[60] Unlike the focus of this book, that study focused on criminal defamation. Criminal Code section 298(1) defines defamatory libel as "published, without justification or excuse, that is likely to injure the reputation of any person by exposing him to hatred, contempt, or ridicule, or that is designed to insult the person of or concerning whom it is published."[61] Lisa Taylor and David Pritchard found that criminal libel prosecutions were rare before widespread adoption of the internet, but they identified approximately four hundred since the beginning of the twenty-first century.[62] The sheer number suggests criminal libel is occurring more frequently than is typically assumed by the legal community.[63] And the increase is decidedly gendered. Taylor and Pritchard found that the dramatic upswing in these cases corresponded with an increase in online slut shaming – the digital shaming of individuals for their (perceived or actual) sexual behaviour.[64] Women who are victimized by this form of harassment can report the experience to the police or launch civil legal proceedings. The high cost of private litigation means that, for some, initiating criminal charges for criminal libel makes more sense when the damages amount to something other than loss of income or wealth.[65] Taylor and Pritchard categorized these cases by drawing on Post's typology of reputation as dignity, as allegations of sexual misconduct are often so socially unacceptable that the individual experiences a loss of self-worth that cannot be evaluated in monetary terms. These findings also align with Pruitt's characterization of new chastity cases as online hate statements that attempt to degrade and humiliate women in relation to their sexuality. At the same time, like traditional chastity cases, the public degradation of women's sexuality reinforces women's association with the private sphere.[66]

Although there is no centralized database for lawsuits, there is reason to believe, via recent media reports, that American women have started initiating lawsuits against men for another gendered iteration of reputational harm. After #MeToo gained popularity, many public figures accused of sexual violence publicly called their accusers liars.[67] In turn, the silence breakers have sued the accused men for discounting their stories of sexual violence.[68] The silence breakers strategically chose a defamation suit because of the statute of limitations in the United States, which prevents the pursuit of other legal options.[69] The list of men currently being sued for calling their accusers liars includes Donald Trump, Bill Cosby, Harvey Weinstein, and Roy Moore.[70] While there is no way to conclude that such lawsuits are widespread, these lawsuits can be seen as a mechanism of resistance by men accused of sexual violence. Their intention is to diminish women's reputations in the public sphere by labelling them as liars.

Defences in Canadian Defamation Law

Defamation law is a profoundly gendered legal category, one centred on normative definitions of masculinity and femininity and the social value of a "good" reputation. Not surprisingly, these masculinist assumptions also permeate the process of defending against a defamation lawsuit. In Canada, a defendant in a defamation suit may rely on a variety of defences, including truth or justification, privilege, fair comment on a matter of public interest, responsible communication on a matter of public interest, reportage, and consent.[71]

The defences of truth, qualified privilege, and fair comment are the most common defences used by silence breakers. Their complexities can make it challenging for silence breakers to navigate silence breaking in ways that protect them from litigation; alternatively, these complexities explain why some silence breakers assume they are protected from litigation. In either case, legal representation by someone with expertise in defamation law is crucial for silence breakers.[72]

Truth and the Option to Countersue

Truth is a complete defence to liability in defamation. If the defendant is going to use truth as a defence, they must prove, on a balance of probabilities, that the contested statement is true.[73] The reason for this defence is that "defamation protects the plaintiff's reputation, and if the plaintiff's reputation is damaged by truth, it is a reputation that is unwarranted and unworthy of protection by the law of defamation."[74] Many of the lawyers I interviewed said that if the defendant pursued this defence, they would likely suggest their client also countersue for sexual violence. One personal-injury lawyer said that a countersuit is a common strategy: "I counter claim for the damages, and that shuts [the plaintiff] down. Now I haven't had any where they've paid me. It's just been a tactic to get rid of the defamation thing."

Another lawyer I spoke to cautioned that there is some risk involved in using truth as a defence and countersuing. Using this strategy means that it's up to the defendant to prove, to the court's satisfaction, that what they said happened was true. The discovery process may require the silence breaker to have intimate details of her private life examined. The lawyer cautioned that this is particularly true if the silence breaker wants to countersue:

> As a complainant in a criminal case, you do have some privacy rights. The defendant has to demonstrate that your therapy records are necessary or required for them to make a full answer in defence. In a civil case, you're asking for money. I'm sorry. Then you have no more right to privacy. That's just how it is. If you're asking the court to give you money for the pain and suffering you've experienced, you are on a level playing field. You have no protection. You chose to come here and do this. You're going to have to open up the books on your emotional well-being. Before, during, and after.

As this lawyer points out, the bulk of the risk involved in drawing on the defence of truth, as well as launching a countersuit, is borne by silence breakers; however, lawsuits can also be risky for the plaintiff – perhaps ironically, their reputation may be further damaged if the court accepts the defence of truth:

> Oftentimes, there will be a defence of truth, which means if it goes to trial, much of the evidence with the trial is going to focus on, Did you do what the defendant said you did? And if there's any possibility that this might have to occur, the plaintiff has to be willing to put all of that evidence out there and be cross-examined on it ... Imagine what the impact might be if you lose because the judge finds the allegations are true.

Although the lawyers saw strategic value in the defence of truth, including initiating a countersuit, the silence breakers I interviewed did not share their enthusiasm, citing the enormous psychological and emotional harms that the process could potentially inflict upon them. When I asked them if they had entertained the possibility of countersuing the plaintiff, two said they were hesitant, fearing that it could be potentially fatal, that going to court could push them to suicide. Elizabeth explained the dilemma further:

> There are days that I want to [countersue]. Then there are days when I'm, like, I can't have … you know [*pause*] descriptions of things in the media. I just don't. You hear these stories about women who are forced to watch the video, or they held up the clothing. I just thought, I don't know if can handle that. I have been so close to suicide so many different times. I'm not sure I'm actually built to withstand the media shit show that will ensue if I sue him. Deep down, I want to, but at the same time, I don't know if I have it in me. As much as I'd love to, I just don't know if I'd survive it.

Catherine had similar fears: "If I had to go to trial with the Superior Court [civil] case, me accusing this person of rape, I was like, this might be the thing that kills me. If I go through the trial and he is found innocent, I will kill myself."

Despite these profound fears, Catherine did eventually threaten the plaintiff with a countersuit after a series of unsuccessful settlement discussions. The threat of the countersuit was, in this case, an effective strategy that led to a settlement agreement between the two parties. Notwithstanding this positive outcome, to prove allegations of sexual violence, women must disclose the most private details of their lives to a plaintiff and potentially in a public court, an experience that can be deeply humiliating and psychologically damaging, making "truth" a difficult defence to access for many silence breakers.

Some of the research participants had misconceptions about truth as a defence. For example, some assumed that if they were telling the truth, especially if they reported the sexual violence to the police, they were safe from legal action. Elizabeth articulated her own misunderstanding:

> So even if you can prove your truth, and you have video, pictures, witnesses, whatever, it is that you need to prove your truth, you still have to go to court and present all that and still have the burden of that lawsuit. I think a lot of people don't understand. They think that they can't even

file [a defamation lawsuit] in the first place if you've told the truth, but that's not how it works.

Elizabeth's quote highlights the reality that even if someone is telling the truth, if a statement of claim is filed, the defendant still must go to court and defend herself. Elizabeth also highlights a common misconception – the assumption that a formal report to the police or a workplace is protected from civil legal action.

Privilege

Privilege is another commonly used legal defence in defamation cases against silence breakers. "Defence of privilege" refers to communications between individuals that are given precedence over the protection of an individual's reputation.[75] For example, once someone has retained legal counsel, their communications with their lawyer are privileged and can't be subjected to litigation. Privilege allows clients to have open communication with their lawyers about their cases. The intent of this defence is to ensure that some communications, specifically those that are shared for a social or moral reason, are excluded from public scrutiny in court.[76] There are two types of privilege: absolute and qualified.[77]

Absolute privilege provides complete immunity from liability for defamation, even if the statement is made with malice. Absolute privilege is narrow and limited to parliamentary proceedings and submissions in provincial legislatures, judicial proceedings, and statements made between legal counsel and their clients.[78] The importance of absolute privilege may be self-evident, the rationale being that some forms of communication are so necessary to the functioning of society that they must be protected from litigation.

In *Caron v A.*, the BC Court of Appeal ruled that reports of sexual assault to the police are not protected by absolute privilege.[79] In November 2012, a youth referred to as "A" by the court reported to the RCMP that Simon Caron had raped her.[80] Caron provided work records, credit card statements, and school attendance records to show that he was in Alberta at the time A claimed the rape occurred. The RCMP dropped the charges laid against Caron. Caron subsequently filed a defamation lawsuit against

A for reporting to the police and for telling people she chose to have the charges dropped. In the statement of claim, Caron cited several consequences that resulted from A telling people that he had been charged and that she had dropped the charges, including his vehicle being vandalized and his friends being threatened.[81] Caron also experienced depression because of the charges, which impacted his work opportunities and caused him to seek out treatment.[82]

A applied to dismiss Caron's claim, arguing that her disclosure to the RCMP should be protected by absolute privilege.[83] Citing public policy research, A argued that failing to protect reports to the police through the framework of absolute privilege would have a chilling effect on future victims' ability or willingness to report their abuse to the appropriate authorities. The BC Court of Appeal rejected these arguments, citing case law that stipulates that absolute privilege is only available to protect complaints made to a quasi-judicial body.[84] Since the police only investigate claims and do not adjudicate them – that is, they do not exercise quasi-judicial or administrative functions – the court ruled that the report falls outside the intended provisions of absolute privilege; therefore, reports made to police are not entitled to these protections.[85]

In light of the court's ruling, it would fall to Parliament to enact legislation to expand the definition of absolute privilege to include reports to the police, something that has yet to occur. This does not mean there are no protections for sexual violence reports to the police. Canadian defendants who report to the police who are then sued for defamation can argue that their report is protected by the defence of qualified privilege.

In comparison to absolute privilege, qualified privilege is more difficult to define because it can potentially apply to a wide range of situations.[86] To claim the protection of qualified privilege, a defendant must satisfy the court that there is a compelling policy reason to permit defamatory statements to be made at the expense of the plaintiff's reputation.[87] As demonstrated in *Hill v Scientology*, the courts take reputational damage very seriously; therefore, the determination of qualified privilege is not taken lightly.[88] Deciding when a communication is protected by qualified privilege is done on a case-by-case basis to determine whether there is a social or moral duty to share information.[89] In *The Law of Torts*, Philip Osborne provides an example of information that may be protected: a parent telling their adult child that the person they are going to marry has engaged in some sort of shameful behaviour.[90] Here, it can be argued that the parent has a moral duty to protect a family member who has a legitimate interest in receiving the information, regardless of the reputational harm it may cause to the object of the communication.

Conversely, the defence of qualified privilege would not extend to a distant friend of the parent telling the adult child the same thing, because they would not be able to demonstrate that they had a duty or interest in sharing the information.[91] Moreover, the courts would need to consider the specific moral and social obligation of the speaker: the defendant can't claim qualified privilege if the impugned statements are made with reckless disregard for the truth, or if there is evidence of malice in making the statements.[92]

As this example demonstrates, whether communications fall under qualified privilege is based on broad principles that allow judges to weigh assessments of social obligations against the social interest to protect reputation. Thus, qualified privilege is a discretionary defence. The courts have ruled that news media outlets are not universally protected by qualified privilege because the media do not have an a priori moral or social duty to report on matters of public interest.[93]

Qualified privilege is a commonly used defence among people sued following a disclosure or report of sexual violence. *Franchuk v Schick* (2014) is one case where the communication was protected by qualified privilege.[94] The plaintiff, Mike Franchuk, was the director of an association where Mary Schick was employed as the sole administrator. Schick wrote a confidential letter to the president of the association stating that Franchuk had sexually harassed her in her office. The letter included direct quotes attributed to Franchuk. Franchuk sued Schick, alleging that the letter was defamatory and false and that he had suffered damages.[95] Schick advanced the defences of truth and qualified privilege.

Because there were no witnesses, the decision depended on the narratives of the two individuals (the one other employee in the office was not present when the alleged sexual harassment occurred). Schick provided diary entries, but the court ruled, "Although the defendant may have written about the alleged incident in her daily diary, that does not make [it] necessarily true, or even more reliable."[96] Further, the decision noted that the other employee in the office testified that she noticed nothing unusual in the interactions between the plaintiff and the defendant that afternoon.[97] Therefore, the court could only rely on the defence of qualified privilege, which was ultimately accepted because the defendant had an interest in making her complaint in writing to the president of the association, who had an interest or duty to receive the letter – an essential element of qualified privilege.[98] Furthermore, the president limited the circulation of the letter to other board members.[99] Therefore, the allegedly defamatory remarks were not widely circulated, thereby protecting the reputation of the plaintiff.

In contrast, the decision in *Whitfield v Whitfield* (2016) revealed the limits of qualified privilege in cases involving disclosures of sexual violence.[100] *Whitfield* established that qualified privilege can be a defence if the defendant discloses sexual violence to certain family members.[101] The decision highlights the limitations of qualified privilege by stating that the defence could not be extended to a communication with the defendant's childhood friend. Agnes Whitfield sued her brother, Bryan Whitfield, for childhood sexual and physical abuse. He countersued for defamation because she sent emails, letters, and postcards to lawyers, former friends, and family members explicitly discussing the abuse. After a twenty-four-day trial spread out over a year, she was awarded $354,200 in damages plus costs.[102] Her brother successfully appealed the decision by challenging the credibility and reliability of an expert witness and Agnes's defence of qualified privilege for the numerous communications she'd had about the abuse.[103] The Ontario Court of Appeal ruled that the trial judge had erred on the question of reliance on an expert witness. More germanely, the court decided that the trial judge erred by applying qualified privilege to all of Agnes Whitfield's communications with third parties.

The court accepted Agnes's defence of qualified privilege for the communications to legal counsel and family but stated that her communications with a high school friend could not be protected. Because Agnes had not been in contact with her old schoolmate for over thirty years, the judge ruled that there was "no duty or interest on the part of the respondent's former high school friend to receive the respondent's communications. In these circumstances, there was no legitimate interest to be protected by the statements."[104] Further, Agnes Whitfield did not testify as to why she copied her friend on the emails, nor was there any evidence to suggest she was seeking advice or support from the friend.[105] In conclusion, the Ontario Court of Appeal ordered Agnes Whitfield to pay $5,000 to her brother for including her childhood friend on the email statements and $50,000 for the cost of the appeal.[106]

Qualified privilege is far more difficult to establish than absolute privilege because the parameters and scope of protection are not clearly defined and are intentionally broad. To date, the courts have not been willing to accept the defence of privilege regarding communications of sexual violence, which will have significant implications for future silence breakers.

Fair Comment

The defence of fair comment on a matter of public interest is intended to restore the balance between free speech and the preservation of reputation. For this defence, there is an important distinction between commentary or opinions and factual statements.[107] Fair comment is most likely to be used by defendants who have been sued for repeating allegations of sexual violence to support the person who disclosed to them or commented publicly on an allegation of sexual violence. For example, research participant Wanda, currently caught up in a lawsuit, mounted the defence of fair comment. The accusations against the plaintiff were widely publicized in the media. Wanda commented about the case on social media. She had never met the accused and had no personal connection to him. For this defence, it is crucial that the defendant was clear to the reader or listener that the statement is the defendant's subjective opinion.[108]

Differentiating between what constitutes commentary or opinion and a factual statement can be challenging. There are five elements for the courts to consider:

1. The comment must be on a matter of public interest.
2. The comment must be based on fact.
3. The comment, though it can include inferences of fact, must be recognizable as a comment.
4. The comment must satisfy the following objective test: Could any person honestly express that opinion on the proven facts?

5. Even if the comment satisfies the objective test, the defence can be defeated if the plaintiff proves that the defendant was actuated by express malice.[109]

Fair comment is intended to allow a great deal of latitude for harsh criticism, to ensure that people are not deterred from participating in the public sphere.[110] The court must also determine that the comment was fair, meaning "the comment was one an honest person could make on the proven facts, however prejudiced, obstinate, or exaggerated his [sic] views may be."[111]

Lawyer Katie Duke examined defamation lawsuits initiated by people who were called racist by antiracism activists in Canada.[112] Here, it's important to note that the experiences of racism and sexual violence are categorically different; however, there are critical commonalities that emerge in the realm of defamation law. For example, like sexual violence, talking about racism is still taboo in Canadian society, and allegations of racist behaviour are often denied or minimized.[113] Also like sexual violence, racism that is more subtle in nature can be difficult to "prove" to the satisfaction of white colonial institutions. When antiracism activists are sued for naming racism, they frequently rely on the defence of fair comment, which Duke argues has several limitations.

The first limitation is the requirement that there be a factual basis for the comment, which has been applied by the courts in a manner that artificially limits the availability of the defence. The Supreme Court of Canada has stated that the facts used to form an opinion must be sufficiently stated or otherwise known to the audience to allow them to come to their own conclusion as to the validity of the opinion.[114] Therefore, to successfully use the defence of fair comment, defendants must either explicitly reference their sources or clearly state that the commentary is their opinion, to allow the receiver of the information to draw their own conclusions.

This requirement fails to take into consideration how people communicate in today's world, particularly on social media platforms or blogs.[115] In *Mainstream Canada v Staniford*, Don Staniford, an activist opposed to salmon farming, was sued for publishing a number of statements on his website comparing salmon farming to the tobacco industry.[116] The court ruled that Staniford was liable: although many of his sources were available on his website, they were not explicitly referenced or hyperlinked.[117] The trial judge ruled that while a "determined reader" could have located the factual basis for his comments, "nondetermined readers" would not be "in a position to evaluate Mr. Staniford's comments."[118] As Duke argues, these links between the "truth" and "fair comment" place unrealistic expectations on those who wish to voice a critical opinion.

The other limitation of the fair comment defence, Duke argues, "is the requirement that the comment meet the objective test of whether 'any person' could 'honestly express that opinion on the proved facts.'"[119] In cases where someone has accused an individual of racism, Duke raises concerns about how the defendant's perspectives on and experiences of racism may be at odds with how racialized people experience racism. Society in general and the law in particular have been unable to grasp that acts of racism are not always blatantly obvious.

Duke's critique is relevant to defamation actions against silence breakers in which there is a divide between how an individual experiences sexual violence (especially when there is no evidence of such acts occurring) and the problematic myths that shape societal beliefs about sexual violence. Furthermore, people who are racialized often experience sexual violence as racialized attacks, which may make proving "fair comment" in a court doubly difficult.

Fair comment is commonly used by silence breakers commenting on allegations of sexual violence or responding to a news media report of sexual violence. As has been demonstrated previously, establishing the "truth" of sexual violence allegations can be challenging given the nature of sexual violence. As with cases involving allegations of racism, many issues stem from the expectation that "any person" would come to the same conclusion.[120] As has been shown, both the courts and the public often make discriminatory and incorrect assumptions about people who disclose or report sexual violence.

Apology and Retraction

In common law, an apology and retraction are mitigating factors in the awarding of damages.[121] Several provincial and territorial defamation acts have codified the apology. For example, in Ontario, the defendant can submit evidence that they made or offered a written apology to the plaintiff before the commencement of legal action. If the action was commenced before the defendant could apologize, they can submit that they did so as soon as they had the opportunity to mitigate the damages.[122]

Some of the silence breakers I interviewed shared that the plaintiff in their cases offered to cease further legal action if they agreed to publicly retract their statement or make a public apology. None of the people I spoke to were willing to do this. But it does happen. For example, I interviewed a journalist who said that she was aware of two women who had been so threatened by litigation that they publicly retracted their statements alleging abuse by former partners.[123] I tried to interview these women to better understand their decision-making process, but neither responded to my interview requests. I share this anecdote because I think it's important to recognize that the threat of litigation can push women to publicly retract their statements, which can have monumental consequences for the individual women and women in general, in that it perpetuates the myth that women often make false claims of violence.

As allegations of sexual violence are at the core of these lawsuits, the defamation proceedings are more likely to resemble a criminal sexual assault trial than a defamation legal proceeding. But, in comparison to a criminal sexual assault trial, the silence breaker has far fewer legal protections. Ultimately, the legal defences available offer limited legal protection for silence breakers and tend to prioritize men's reputation over women's ability to express themselves safely. This is one reason research participants were fearful of having their cases proceed to trial. Many of the research participants were also aware that the legal proceedings would be shaped by stereotypes about people who report sexual violence, along with other discriminatory stereotypes.

The concepts of (male) reputation as property and reputation as dignity put forward by Robert Post are useful for understanding what is at stake in these cases.[124] First and foremost, the identification of reputation as a form of property explains why pecuniary damages are usually sought: the assumption is that reputational damage negatively impacts men's ability to participate in the market.[125] As my research reveals, however, financial loss tells only part of the story: in many cases, the plaintiffs are also seeking vindication from the court on the grounds they were wrongfully accused of sexual violence. Here, the concept of reputation as dignity is highly relevant. These men are also seeking redemption so they can re-enter social spaces from which they may have been excluded.[126]

At the same time, it's worth noting that the lawsuit will not always vindicate men's reputations. There are risks associated with pursuing this legal route. As one defamation lawyer pointed out, the court may accept the silence breaker's version of events. Further, the lawsuit may bring more public attention to the allegations. While the lawsuit is harmful to the silence breaker regardless, it does not always necessarily redeem the plaintiff's reputation in the eyes of others. In fact, a lawsuit may cause further damage to his reputation.

This insight raises more questions about the motivations for such lawsuits. As I argue in the chapters to follow, the allure of legal action for men accused of sexual violence includes its punitive effects on the silence breaker in ways that mimic the abusive dynamics that ground the allegations in the first place.

3

Sick and Silenced

The silence breakers interviewed reported a wide range of consequences that they attributed to being sued. For many silence breakers, the silencing effect of the litigation directly affects their emotional and physical health. Most reported experiencing severe depression and anxiety, even after the litigation ended. A few also tied the stress of the litigation to physical symptoms such as chronic pain. Many of the silence breakers found the censorship of the litigation to be a key contributor to their stress. They were unable to talk to anyone, even trusted friends and family, about what had occurred, and many identified the silencing as contributing to a wider political silencing of sexual violence. Litigation has the ability to push sexual violence discourse from the public sphere, including formal reports to police or other institutions. If these lawsuits continue, we may witness the disappearance of sexual violence discourse altogether.

Being Sued: A Somatic Experience

Many silence breakers I spoke with developed significant physical and mental health problems after being sued or threatened with a lawsuit. Within Heidi Rimke's psychocentrism framework, psychological distress and struggles are understood as being socially structured rather than "defects of abnormal individuals."[1] The psychological and physical illnesses that silence breakers experience cannot and must not be individualized or depoliticized.[2] I reject the notion that the research participants' symptoms can be separated from the antitherapeutic impacts of the legal system and other modes of institutional retaliation. They are symptoms of a patriarchal society in which men can strategically use a legal system that fundamentally disbelieves women and other institutional mechanisms to abuse and inflict additional harm on their victims. The mental, emotional, and physical consequences of sexual violence are well documented.[3] Legal retaliation can compound its already debilitating impacts. It's no surprise that the research participants who reported experiencing the most severe health consequences were those who had experienced sexual violence. But bystanders who were sued also experienced a series of health problems that they linked to the stress of their lawsuits and systemic injustices.

Emotional Distress

The feminist literature on betrayal trauma is a useful framework for understanding how both individual abusers and institutions can exacerbate the trauma of sexual violence.[4] Sexual violence is frequently intertwined with betrayal. At an individual level, this occurs if the perpetrator is in a position of trust – for example, an intimate partner, a family member, or a friend.[5] When an institution is involved and fails or has failed to intervene or respond appropriately to sexual violence, silence breakers frequently report experiencing heightened betrayal, or "institutional betrayal."[6]

For example, campus community members often develop trust for and dependency on the university through interpersonal relationships. They may view their university as a safe space that cares about their well-being.[7] After reporting sexual violence to the university only to have their report denied or their experience minimized, they may feel institutional betrayal. The institutional betrayal may be severe if the institution failed to prevent the sexual violence, for example, by allowing a faculty member known to sexually harass students to continue teaching. Institutional betrayal often coincides with higher levels of several posttraumatic symptoms and psychological distress, which exacerbates the trauma of being sexually assaulted.[8] For example, women reported experiencing heightened anxiety, disassociation, and trauma-specific sexual symptoms.[9]

Nearly all the silence breakers reported experiencing anxiety, depression, and suicidal ideation.[10] For those who experienced sexual violence, a lawsuit hindered their ability to heal. Elizabeth explained: "I'm going to use the words of my counsellor. She said it's like trying to heal burns when you are standing in the fire … That's sort of where it is. Everything I've had to do has been coping mechanisms and survival. I can't even peel back any of the layers and get to the actual trauma." Even though years had passed since Elizabeth learned of the lawsuit, she continued to experience emotional distress:

> I was in such a trauma state. When I was in the midst of it, I just kept going, "Oh, tomorrow will be better. Next week will be better." I kept waiting for that ... you know, how sometimes you go through [a] couple weeks, or [a] couple days where you feel shitty, and then you get up and you have this renewed energy ... Well, I anticipated that that was going to happen. Any day now. And here I am four years, five years, later, right? And that's been hard, too, just realizing that that is not happening. I just keep waiting for it to end.

Others shared Elizabeth's experience of extended trauma. The notoriously slow pace of the legal system, including delays in proceedings, was cited as a common cause of distress among participants, who were retraumatized each time they were forced to relive the sexual violence and then had their experiences denied and minimized by their abuser and the legal system.

This sense of never-ending trauma led a number of women to have suicidal thoughts. Camila disclosed:

> I have been in really bad places. It is so difficult to get through living and finding a will to live without the added layer of someone trying to tell you it isn't real and it's defamatory and your experience is invalid and you're a Jane Doe – some corpse that no one has identified. That is so ... it really reinforces ... nihilistic and suicidal impulses. That is the biggest danger of it.

For some, suicidal ideation continued even after the legal matter was concluded. Catherine, who reached a settlement agreement, told me she continues to feel suicidal because what happened fundamentally changed her perspective on the world: "I am still suicidal. I'm out of danger, but [*cries*] the thing that fucks me the most is knowing that I live in a world where this happens, where this could happen to so many vulnerable people. The world is not equipped to help us, or even believe us."

As I have argued previously, suicide and suicidal ideation are often framed within psy-discourses of individual pathology and mental illness. But viewing disclosures of suicidal ideation within this framing ignores the numerous forms of structural and systemic violence individuals experience that can *make* people *want* to die.[11] The more concerning element is how the legal system can be used strategically by abusive men to inflict such incredible emotional distress upon others that they consider ending their lives to escape the harms of the legal proceedings.

Physical Health

Beyond psychological and emotional distress, four of the research participants shared with me that they'd developed physical health problems. Two had chronic pain, and two developed severe digestion issues during their legal battles that went on for years. Medical research has found that adult abuse survivors are at risk of developing a wide range of long-term negative health outcomes, including an increased likelihood of disease, because of the chronic stress associated with sexual violence.[12] One silence breaker, Tamara, developed a range of health problems that she attributed to the stress of having to constantly defend her victimization in numerous legal and quasi-legal forums: "I go through really severe blows, and it's showing up in my body now. Not being able to let go. I am going for ovarian tests now, sore, lasting for months, and I was diagnosed with GERD, which is gastro-oesophageal reflux disease, but I am convinced it is all the stress. I can't digest anymore."

Olivia, a journalist, investigated the widespread abuse of Indigenous children by a white man in a position of power. After the story was published, the man she wrote about sued her, and she countersued him for defamation for discrediting her reporting. During the legal proceedings, Olivia developed severe digestion issues and lost fifteen pounds. Olivia linked her health problems to witnessing numerous institutional failures to protect Indigenous women and children:

> What I saw was a machine that protects a guy. Like, there are sixty-five people now who have told me about his abuse. Either it happened to them, they witnessed it, or they reported it. Sixty-five. I saw the machinery. I think what really got my gut and my inability to digest food now

was how well the machinery works to protect someone who people have said is an extremely violent man towards women and children.

For Olivia, witnessing how colonialism and patriarchal laws worked to protect a white man in a position of power literally made her sick.

Several of the silence breakers likewise addressed how witnessing institutional responses to sexual violence challenged their perceptions of personal safety and justice. Catherine stated:

> I think my feelings of safety and integration with the world, which were already pretty fucked up, definitely got worse. I think, after a time, I had to just stop fighting, because my body was shutting down. So as much as I would love to continue pursuing legal options and trying to find a way, not only to find justice but also to protect other people, I just can't right now. And it's very hard to accept that. But I need to rest and heal and maybe find some other way to exist in the world.

Individual Silencing

At the individual level, (most) lawyers will tell anyone involved in any type of lawsuit not to talk about the lawsuit or what led to the legal action with anyone but them. For silence breakers, this instruction can result in loneliness and isolation. A significant trauma has now been rendered unspeakable. Lawyers also recommend that silence breakers make their social media accounts private. In theory, this is good advice because it limits the information that a plaintiff can use to discredit the allegations or the silence breaker as a "legitimate" victim. In cases of sexual violence, if a complainant's behaviour does not align with that of the ideal victim, her choices, rather than the abusive behaviour, will be scrutinized.[13] Knowing this, lawyers have an obligation to advise silence breakers to minimize their public presence to reduce the material a plaintiff can acquire to discredit her. While this advice is standard for both parties in any type of legal proceeding, in cases of gendered violence, there are specific and concerning societal and individual implications.

Feminist activists and scholars globally have used social media as a tool for advancing gender equality.[14] Such movements have highlighted the power of social media to amplify narratives of sexual violence to an extent that would not have been possible for previous generations.[15] New digital media challenges "old media" in that it disrupts the hierarchy of content creation, allowing those without a platform to create and disseminate content, thereby expanding the ability of people, specifically women and girls, to engage in the public sphere and to contribute in meaningful ways to public discussions about gendered violence.[16] Online spaces can be powerful for silence breakers because they can receive information, participate in public debate, have a voice, and receive validation and vindication, in addition to controlling their narrative and holding offenders accountable.[17] This was true for the silence breakers in this study, many of whom used social media for several purposes, including for support, as a way to receive validation, or to voice concern about the way the police or their workplace responded to their report of sexual violence.

While online spaces can empower silence breakers, feminist researchers caution that technology can also be used as a weapon by abusive men.[18] It offers a platform for abusive men to continue their sexual harassment, abuse, and violence in the digital sphere.[19] Before their individual lawsuits, some of the participants used social media to connect with online communities following their experiences of violence. But the use of social media also opened them up to additional surveillance by the men who abused them and their allies, leading to a lawsuit or the threat of a lawsuit. For example, prior to the legal action against her, Catherine was an active user of the now-defunct social media platform Tumblr. For Catherine, Tumblr provided a supportive online network that connected her with others experiencing the aftermath of violence. She talked about how the various legal retaliations she experienced took away a crucial support network and forced her into silence:

> I used to publish a lot of my life online, and I didn't feel able to do that after [the lawsuit]. So, I didn't have access to my Tumblr blog anymore because [the defendant] had taken screenshots of it, also because their friends were following it and sometimes posting things I say in other places. Just felt like surveillance all the time.

The surveillance of Catherine's online activities was distressing and invasive. Like Catherine, Camila told me that she knew her abuser was monitoring her social media account, which felt like an extension of the abuse she'd endured during their relationship. "I had a couple of weirdly not overtly or threatening emails from [ex-partner] saying that he was looking at what I was saying and warning that he was surveilling my social media. I got worried about what he would do."

Shortly after, Camila's ex-partner initiated legal action. But he did not serve Camila, which put her in legal limbo. Knowing that he is watching her online activity and that he can amend the claim to include new allegations of defamation and serve her with the lawsuit at any moment, Camila self-censors what she puts on social media.

Since many of the interview participants referenced their online activities, I was curious about what they thought of the #MeToo movement. Camila and Elizabeth acknowledged that while they were grateful that the public discussion on sexual violence was happening, they felt excluded because they knew that their online interactions were under surveillance and could lead to further legal consequences. Camila said: "Seeing the conversation going on helps in some way, and the other side of that is that I can't participate as much as I want to. I can't be part of that conversation because of the law in Canada and how this stuff works and that lawsuit sitting out there." Here, Camila references the plaintiff-friendly nature of defamation law in Canada, which she felt would fail to protect her if she were to participate in the #MeToo discussion. Elizabeth shared a similar sentiment: "I cannot speak because it might make the lawsuit worse. I cannot go on Twitter and do #MeToo. I cannot do any of these things because it puts me in a more vulnerable position. And it drives me nuts that this happened to me, and I can't even talk about it. Kills me." Camila and Elizabeth demonstrate that although the #MeToo movement has amplified discourse surrounding sexual violence, not all survivors have been afforded the privilege of participating. Both women expressed that their exclusion from the #MeToo discourse had a profound impact on their well-being.

The silence breakers noted that lawsuits often had a chilling effect on allies and activists who feared being sued. For example, research participant Wanda was being sued for a social media post she wrote in response to news reporting on a high-profile sexual violence case. Wanda felt that, despite the consequences she personally faced, the possibility of a lawsuit should not deter other people from speaking out about sexual violence. Wanda criticized some of her peers in the antiviolence movement who had retreated into silence:

> The extent that people internalize that they are not going to say anything negative ever because, think of the cost. Watching people warn each other – don't say this thing – it is just gross. It gets in the way of addressing problems. There will always be people who are powerful who do bad things – afraid of transparency. That has been infuriating.

Wanda spoke about her frustration with others in the antiviolence movement, especially those in positions of power and privilege who remain silent out of fear of legal action. She correctly noted that this fear is a major obstacle to addressing sexual violence.

Janet, a private-practice lawyer who specializes in sexual abuse litigation, expressed a similar frustration. In one case she consulted on, the clients were parents of a child who was being assaulted at school. The parents were warned by others that if they reported, they could be sued for defamation:

> People had said, "You can't tell people about [the abuse]. You will be sued for defamation." What? Everyone knows it went on. That is absurd. You can be sued for defamation – but – people trot that out as if that is the answer to the question or an insurmountable obstacle, or a high probability in certain circumstances when it's a low probability.

Janet tied fear of legal action as a deterrent to reporting sexual violence to a lack of public knowledge about civil claims more generally. She suggested that rape crisis centres and sexual assault centres should be educated about civil litigation and how to discuss and report sexual violence in a manner that would reduce the likelihood of a successful defamation action. As she rightly notes, the possibility of a lawsuit should not deter bystanders from taking action to prevent and respond to sexual violence in their communities.

For both Janet and Wanda, the bigger concern is the possibility that advocates will self-censor and be less willing to take action to stop sexual violence. Being afraid to speak will only serve to protect people in positions of power and make targets of sexual violence more vulnerable to abuse. Neither Janet nor Wanda attempted to minimize the significant consequences of being sued; in fact, Wanda spoke at length about the tremendous cost the lawsuit had on her financially and emotionally. Her legal bills were nearing $100,000, with no end in sight.[20]

Rather, their interventions aligned with a theme that emerged among other research participants, especially bystanders. Many of these participants cited their social and institutional privilege. They felt they had a moral duty to protect and support those with less privilege. Even knowing what they do now, they would act the same way. The faculty I interviewed said that while their lawsuits were emotionally draining and damaging to their academic careers, they did not regret supporting individuals who occupied positions of far less privilege.

Of course, those who I spoke with felt safe enough to speak to me. I couldn't capture the voices of those who were too afraid to speak to me or those who pre-emptively chose not to speak about sexual violence out of fear of a retaliatory lawsuit. It's impossible to capture the magnitude of the silencing effect these lawsuits can have on sexual violence discourse.

The Violence of the Gag Order

A gag order – more formally referred to as a nondisclosure agreement, or NDA – is a legal order that limits future speech or action as agreed upon by the two parties. Most gag orders have no time limitations and are unlimited in scope, forbidding the parties from disclosing anything about what led to the litigation or the settlement.[21] A major challenge in studying such agreements is that "there is neither a requirement nor a legal compulsion to reveal the outcomes, if one or more parties prefer to keep the matter private."[22] For the participants I spoke with, gag orders caused tremendous pain. This pain is the reason I use the term "gag order" as opposed to the more neutral "nondisclosure agreement": "gag order" recognizes the somatic and political harm of such agreements as a mechanism of violence. For silence breakers, gag orders are not so much agreements as they are something they were forced to accept, often by their own lawyers. To gag someone because of a lack of other options, without their full consent, is inherently violent.

Gag orders are commonly used in settlement agreements in a wide range of contexts.[23] As discussed in Chapter 1, there are many reasons why both parties may wish to settle the lawsuit out of court, including the significant costs tied to litigation and keeping certain facts of the case out of the public realm.[24] Gag orders are often presented as if they are there to protect the privacy of people who experienced sexual violence.[25] In reality, there is little evidence to suggest that gag orders are beneficial for silence breakers; rather, they benefit social institutions and help the person accused of sexual violence escape public scrutiny. Sara Ahmed's research on sexual and racial violence complaints at universities found that many women signed gag orders in exchange for money or other benefits such as a sabbatical. For this reason, Ahmed argues that gag orders are frequently a form of bribery. She defines a bribe as "a gift that is intended to influence action corruptly."[26] The silence breaker is awarded for retreating into silence.

Silence breakers told me they felt pressured by their lawyers to agree to a gag order because the lawyer believed that they couldn't settle without one and that going to trial would be financially risky. Over a decade ago, Ontario's Cornwall Public Inquiry raised concerns about the legal expectation that survivors of sexual violence remain silent about the abuse they experienced.[27] The inquiry's final report detailed the numerous systemic failures of the legal system and other public institutions in responding to allegations of childhood sexual abuse in Cornwall, Ontario.[28] The report concluded that including confidentiality agreements in legal settlements created additional harm for survivors: "For survivors of sexual abuse, and where secrecy and shame are part of their injury, having to maintain silence in return for a payment can have very negative consequences."[29]

The report noted that gag orders were most often boilerplate legal agreements that failed to take into consideration the unique needs of people who experienced sexual violence.[30] For example, some of the agreements suggested that a person cannot discuss a settlement with anyone, including spouses or counsellors – a clause potentially detrimental to the well-being of sexual violence survivors.[31] The inquiry recommended that individuals should be able to discuss their experience of abuse and the settlement without limitations while allowing for protection with respect to the quantum of payment or the identity of the victim, if that is what the victim wanted.[32] In early 2023, the Canadian Bar Association passed a resolution with 94 percent support to reduce the use of nondisclosure agreements to silence whistle-blowers and victims of sexual violence. Further, the association has resolved to lobby all levels of the Canadian government to act on the misuse of nondisclosure agreements in these cases.[33]

The women I spoke with had similar concerns about the long-term impact a gag order would have on their recovery, not to mention the consequences of being prohibited from shining a light on systemic failures. They didn't regard gag orders as an agreement between two equal parties. Instead, they perceived that the unequal power dynamics between themselves and their abusers had forced them into silence.

Both Bonnie Robichaud and Laura accepted gag orders. Neither of the settlements they received was tied to the lawsuits examined in this study but instead to actions they took against their workplaces, which they felt were liable for the sexual violence they had experienced. They spoke to me about their gag orders and cautioned against them. In the 1980s, Bonnie Robichaud agreed to what she called a "secret agreement" with her workplace.[34] The workplace would pay for her to attend university with a three-year leave from her job. In exchange, Robichaud had to abandon her workplace complaints and abandon her attempt to seek damages from the man who sexually harassed her. Once she was done school, she would be employed in another department.

Laura, like many survivors, had experienced multiple instances of sexual violence, including at a previous workplace. Laura took legal action against the previous organization she worked for, resulting in her signing a strict gag order in exchange for $15,000. At the time of the interview, Laura deeply regretted accepting the settlement: "I actually developed symptoms where my face would go numb, and I was having all these throat issues. I was having physical symptoms of feeling gagged. I was working on that in therapy, and I realized a lot of it was stemming from [the gag order]. Actually was gagged." This experience deterred her from agreeing to another gag order when she again experienced sexual violence: "I ended up getting offered a settlement. Like, it was pretty substantial. It was $60,000, which almost would bankrupt their company, probably. They were desperate to shut me up. But they refused to settle with me without a gagging clause. I said, 'Under no circumstances will I sign one.'"[35]

In an interview, Robichaud echoed Laura, saying that the confidentiality requirement "puts more insult on big injury." One of the motivating factors for Robichaud in seeking leave at the Supreme Court of Canada was to make the terms of the agreement public. Robichaud told me she wanted to share publicly what had happened to her and to seek a larger systemic remedy: "As long as it is a secret, we don't know about it. We can't study them."

The lawyers interviewed for this study offered a range of opinions on whether gag orders should be used and in what circumstances. While some were adamant that a legal settlement could not happen without a gag order, others said they often advised clients against a gag order that was overly broad in scope. While their opinions diverged, they were all cognizant of the emotional consequences of gag orders for silence breakers.

This recognition of the potential harms may be a result of the participant selection process – I mostly spoke to lawyers with extensive experience working with clients who had experienced sexual violence. They agreed that lawyers inexperienced in sexual violence litigation may be unaware that gag orders may cause further harm to the silence breaker. This lack of understanding was confirmed by several research participants, who told me they had worked with lawyers who lacked a political analysis of sexual violence and who advised them to agree to the gag order because it was "standard practice" in civil litigation.

A long-time sexual abuse litigator, Darlene, questioned whether gag orders could even be enforced. It may be difficult to prove that a defendant has breached the settlement. The victim will likely not have the money to pay damages. The courts may be unwilling to uphold such an agreement as a matter of public policy:

> It's very rare that I see anyone even attempt a traditional gag order. If they do, I just laugh at them and say, "First of all, I don't think it will ever be enforceable." I think they're void as [they are] against public policy. Now there's no case that says that, but I would be very happy to argue the first case of that issue. That's ridiculous.

Laura's experience suggests Darlene could be correct. Laura told me that she eventually became so frustrated with the way the gag order negatively affected her healing process that she decided to disregard the terms of the settlement entirely. She began speaking openly about what happened to her, including the role the institution played in keeping her quiet. At the time of the interview, the organization had not pursued a breach of settlement.

The above legal opinion, however, was not shared by all the lawyers. Jessica, another lawyer specializing in sexual violence litigation, told me she found that plaintiffs so often request terms of secrecy that gag orders are unavoidable during settlement negotiations. Despite this, Jessica noted there is room for creativity, especially if the allegations are already in the public domain. She shared the specifics of a nondisclosure agreement she'd negotiated:

> A lawyer experienced some pretty heinous sexual harassment by a pretty senior lawyer, and we negotiated this ridiculous multistage NDA. I basically said to the other side, "She is in the early years of her career. How does she continue to work in this industry for the next forty years and remain silent about what happened to her as an articling student? And what if she is a senior partner in the next twenty years on a panel and she gets asked, 'Did you ever experience this?' She has to be tight-lipped about the whole encounter in her work." We ended up negotiating things. She can never name him. She can name who the employer was at the time. After five years, she can talk about the fact that she experienced sexual harassment by a senior lawyer during her career, or something like that.

It is possible to negotiate a creative settlement in cases of sexual violence, one that will not entirely silence the silence breaker. In fact, many of the lawyers experienced in sexual abuse litigation seemed to follow the recommendation made by the Cornwall Public Inquiry to ensure that gag orders are not overly broad.[36]

But, as mentioned previously, not all silence breakers have lawyers knowledgeable about how sexual violence litigation is fundamentally different from standard personal-injury litigation such as motor vehicle claims. Lawyers representing silence breakers need to be aware of the potential long-term psychological distress and other physical health concerns a gag order may cause a silence breaker if the terms of the agreement make her afraid to speak about sexual violence entirely, especially to counsellors, supportive friends, and family members.

The silence breakers I spoke to cited fear of being forced to sign a gag order if they couldn't afford to take the case to court. Bonnie Robichaud and Laura experienced profoundly adverse impacts on their well-being because they agreed to a gag order. Both women resisted and fought the gag order once they realized it was hindering their political activism and healing process. Many of the silence breakers who faced legal action or a legal threat cited concern that the possibility of a gag order could impact their personal-healing journey. They also worried that the inability to speak openly about sexual violence would hinder the antiviolence movement.

Clearly, gag orders arising from retaliatory lawsuits function to censor the speech of silence breakers. For example, Laura and Robichaud, who both signed gag orders relating to workplace sexual violence, challenged their gag orders when they recognized their individual and systemic consequences. While Robichaud went to the courts to argue that she should not be silenced, Laura simply started speaking about what happened to her, despite the gag order. Wanda and Janet encouraged bystanders to not allow a potential lawsuit to deter them from addressing sexual violence within their communities.

Media Libel Chill

Defamation suits silence more than individuals. Lawsuits and the fear of litigation have a palpable effect on traditional media outlets and journalists and how they report on stories of sexual violence. Holding back on publishing or broadcasting stories out of fear of being sued is known as "libel chill." The Supreme Court of Canada addressed libel chill in *WIC Radio Ltd v Simpson*:

> There is concern that matters of public interest go unreported because publishers fear the ballooning cost and disruption of defending a defamation action. Investigative reports get "spiked," it is contended, because, while true, they are based on facts that are difficult to establish according to rules of evidence. When controversies erupt, statements of claim often follow as night follows day, not only in serious claims ... but in actions

launched simply for the purpose of intimidation. "Chilling" false and defamatory speech is not a bad thing in itself, but chilling debate on matters of legitimate public interest raises issues of inappropriate censorship and self-censorship. Public controversy can be a rough trade, and the law needs to accommodate its requirements.[37]

In a study of Canadian newspaper coverage of domestic violence, Bailey Gerrits found that journalists and editors consider the possibility of a libel lawsuit when they decide whether to report on a case of domestic violence. The editorial decision is often guided by whether there is an element of public interest – for example, if there is a potential public safety issue such as other people being at risk of being victimized by the alleged perpetrator. As a result, reports of gendered violence may be omitted from the news because of the perceived limitations of the libel defences available to the media and, more specifically, in matters of public interest and fair comment.[38]

Despite the Supreme Court of Canada's broad warnings about the democratic hazards of "chilling debate on matters of legitimate public interest," recent developments have made the mainstream media more concerned about libel than ensuring that stories about gender violence get told. For example, when the *Toronto Star* published a story about a boxing gym for women who had experienced violence, they featured the story of a member but did not seek comment on her allegations of abuse against her ex-husband. Even though he was not named in the piece, the husband threatened legal action for defamation.[39] The threat led to the editors revising the story on the grounds that it did not meet the *Star*'s editorial standard of fairness, which states, "*The Star* is obligated to obtain and publish all sides of any story it reports. Before publication, every effort must be made to present subjects with all accusations." The digital story now includes a disclaimer indicating that although the man was not named in the story, he was not given an opportunity to respond to allegations, as he should have been before the article was published.[40] If news outlets are hesitant to label a woman a "survivor" in a story that does not name the perpetrator out of fear of possible litigation, even if the central facet of the story is not necessarily about the allegations, sexual violence could risk being pushed out of mainstream media or result in a vague or watered-down version of what happened to avoid litigation.

One lawyer I interviewed, who specializes in sexual abuse litigation, noticed a distinct shift in media outlets' willingness to publish stories about allegations of sexual violence following the #MeToo movement. This lawyer felt the media's reluctance was tied to fear of litigation. Prior to #MeToo, news outlets regularly allowed people who had experienced sexual violence to remain anonymous in the story. After, the media was far less likely to allow people anonymity. For example, at the time of the interview, she was working on a case that involved numerous women who had experienced sexual violence in the workplace in a small Canadian city. The women wanted the media to report on their working conditions, but they wanted to remain anonymous out of fear of retaliation. The media outlet refused to publish the story; as a result, the sexual harassment litigation against the company was unknown to the public.

Media outlets' fear of litigation is legitimate. In the last several years, there have been several lawsuits against them following the publication of a story or article about sexual violence allegations. For example, former Ontario Progressive Conservative Party leader Patrick Brown sued several media entities and people responsible for publishing a story alleging his "sexual misconduct."[41] A Canadian poet and former editor filed a $13.5 million lawsuit against the *Globe and Mail* and *Toronto Star* and four unidentified women.[42] The story reporting the lawsuit indicated that a separate lawsuit would be filed against *BuzzFeed News*.[43]

If media outlets are sued, freelance authors are in a unique predicament and are far less likely to receive any support from the news outlet. Indigenous author Alicia Elliott published an article in *Flare* magazine about her experience of libel chill and the unique challenges for freelance authors.[44] Elliott wrote about her decision to pull an editorial about numerous historical sexual violence allegations made by Indigenous people against a white man in a position of power.[45] She decided to pull the story after she learned that the news outlet wanted to run the story without having it checked by a lawyer.[46] Without that added protection, Elliott's own fears of legal action set in; as a freelance writer, she was especially concerned that a lawsuit could financially devastate her and her family.[47]

Even if a story is checked by a lawyer prior to publication, litigation can still be commenced. For example, Marilou McPhedran wrote an article about physicians sexually abusing their patients for the *Globe and Mail*. Even though the article was reviewed by the *Globe*'s legal team, she was sued by the Ontario Medical Association (OMA). In an interview with me, McPhedran shared that when she was first sued, the *Globe* refused to help her pay for a lawyer to defend herself:

> The OMA only sued me for the op-ed in the *Globe*. That op-ed had been lawyered by the *Globe*, by the *Globe* experts. They approved it for publication. But ... the OMA ... sued only me and the *Globe* said, "Oh, good luck with that." Good luck with that? They lawyered it. They approved it. They published it. They let me hang.[48]

Eventually, the *Globe* provided her with financial support, but only after it faced pressure to assist her with her legal defence from an editor at the *Toronto Star*. The *Globe and Mail* provided $100,000 with the caveat that it got to choose the lawyer.[49] As discussed earlier, the OMA lawsuit against McPhedran silenced her and other advocates. During and after the five-year lawsuit, other media outlets became reluctant to publish stories about the original issue in contention – sexual violence of patients by regulated medical professionals.[50]

A lawsuit has significant consequences for those being sued. The most obvious is the financial cost. But the silence breakers I spoke with also disclosed that they'd developed mental and physical health problems, tied to the stress of the retaliation, after being sued. Physical symptoms were exacerbated by the expectation of silence as these women lost control of their narratives. Once a lawsuit is initiated, lawyers often tell their clients to stop talking about what happened to them – advice that may be legally beneficial but can also be detrimental to the victim's well-being. The censorship not only impacts individual silence breakers, but it also systematically contributes to the silencing of sexual violence discourse in the public sphere. In short, fear of retaliatory litigation could result in the reprivatization of discourse about sexual violence.

4

Campus Sexual Violence

A surprising number of silence breakers in this study are tied to sexual violence at postsecondary institutions, and their abusers invoked their university's complaint processes in addition to a defamation lawsuit. This chapter focuses on the experiences of silence breakers who attempted to challenge campus sexual violence and hold perpetrators accountable. The university's response to sexual violence must be situated within a neoliberal ethos of university branding that seeks to preserve the institution's reputation. The universities' failure to prevent and respond to sexual violence makes silence breakers vulnerable to retaliatory lawsuits from faculty members.

Over the last several years in Canada, there has been a growing number of cases where faculty members accused of sexual violence have been terminated from their positions. At face value, these terminations can be regarded as a favourable outcome for those who reported the sexual violence. Yet, as the two cases discussed in Chapter 1 show, they leave the silence breaker vulnerable to retaliation in the form of lawsuits.[1] There have been other instances of faculty suing students, such as the (now former) McGill professor who sued a student and a faculty member for $600,000. He claimed that the "affair" he had with a student had been consensual and alleged that the women had a "vendetta" against him and were engaged in a "ruthless smear campaign" to have him fired.[2] A former University of Windsor law professor sued his colleague Julie Macfarlane when she disclosed to a university in Trinidad that he had faced several allegations, including sexual harassment, that led to his termination from the University of Windsor.³ Taken together, these cases raise important questions about campus sexual violence, the ramifications of the university's response, and how individuals are too frequently left to bear the burden of retaliation without institutional support. As Sara Ahmed aptly notes, there is often a gap between experience and appearance in university responses to sexual violence. By delving into this process, we learn about institutional mechanics and how institutions work.⁴ The silence breakers' narratives reveal a counternarrative about how sexual violence is responded to on campus.

None of the silence breakers interviewed were sued by students accused of sexual violence, but this can happen. In 2020, a McGill student accused of sexual violence sued the university, the student newspaper, two student organizations, and his accuser for $1.5 million.⁵ But, to date, this case appears to be an anomaly. Most lawsuits are initiated by faculty members rather than students. The seeming increase in lawsuits against silence breakers over the last decades coincides with international conversations about campus sexual violence.

There has been a resurgence in feminist study and activism addressing campus sexual violence.⁶ This has led to growing public pressure, which has caused universities to implement new educational campaigns about consent, stand-alone sexual violence policies, and sexual violence centres. Despite these efforts, campus sexual violence has not declined since it was first identified as a widespread issue in the 1980s and 1990s.⁷ There is also plenty of evidence to suggest that despite numerous initiatives, university administrators and the new sexual violence policies have failed those who report campus sexual violence.⁸ Sexual violence policies are often difficult to navigate, and sexual violence offices are frequently more for optics than empowered with the ability to provide institutional support to those who want to make a report.⁹

While I interviewed a disproportionate number of people who faced retaliation after a faculty member was accused of sexual violence, it is impossible to state that university faculty are more likely to sue or retaliate than men outside of academia. I expect that there is a disproportionate number of faculty represented in this study for several reasons. First, academics likely value research more than nonacademics, which may have prompted them to participate. Second, as mentioned, nearly all the research participants with ties to campus had a background in social justice organizing, which may have led them to take a more active role in responding to sexual violence. Third, the university's hierarchal structure provides abusive men in positions of authority with more opportunities to meet women, many of whom are younger. The power dynamics in the university are enormous, especially when students depend on faculty for jobs or reference letters.[10]

This isn't to suggest that campus sexual violence or such lawsuits targeting campus community members who speak out about sexual violence are necessarily a new problem on campus. The earliest defamation lawsuit regarding allegations of sexual violence I was able to find during this research was filed in the early 1980s, after a group of women journalism students at Carleton University held a press conference denouncing sexual harassment in their department.[11] In turn, three male professors in the department sued the women, alleging that "their failure to name names has damaged the reputation of all the faculty teachers."[12]

In my interview with Constance Backhouse, she recalled similar incidents in the late 1980s and early '90s when women faculty members across the country began releasing chilly climate reports on gender discrimination, sexual harassment, and racism in their university departments. The feminist academics involved in writing the reports published an edited collection of them titled *Breaking Anonymity* to document a number of perspectives.[13] In the introduction, the editors wrote that they made the editorial decision to exclude one of the reports because its authors were being threatened with a defamation lawsuit.[14] A group of male professors from that department had already initiated a lawsuit against a media outlet for broadcasting the report's release.[15] Backhouse, who was one of the women involved in writing the reports, told me that the media outlet had contacted her for legal background on the issue, but she never heard from them again or learned of the outcome.[16] Nonetheless, the lawsuit silenced as it was intended to – the chilly climate report at the centre of the legal action was then removed from the book.

Campus Sexual Assault in Canada

A 2019 survey found that 71 percent of postsecondary students reported that they had witnessed or experienced unwanted sexual behaviour.[17] More worrisome is that 11 percent of women students experienced a sexual assault, and 45 percent reported at least one unwanted sexualized behaviour in the previous twelve months. In comparison, only 4 percent of male students reported a sexual assault while 32 percent reported an unwanted sexualized behaviour.[18] In total, 197,000 women stated that they had been sexually assaulted at some point during their postsecondary education, a rate three times higher than their male counterparts.[19] As discussed, sexual violence can result in a range of psychological and emotional consequences for the survivor. For students, it can negatively impact their academic life. It changes how safe they perceive the campus to be, and it negatively impacts their studies. Respondents reported skipping classes, asking for extensions, and dropping classes.[20]

There has been renewed public pressure on universities and colleges to implement sexual violence policies and prevention programs.[21] Since 2016, provinces including Ontario, British Columbia, Quebec, and Manitoba have passed legislation mandating all postsecondary institutions that receive public funds must implement stand-alone sexual violence policies.[22] By 2017, postsecondary institutions across the country had released new sexual violence policies, and many created sexual violence offices.[23] While many of these sexual violence offices are staffed by feminist activists, to varying degrees, the universities have co-opted feminist language to discuss sexual violence. For example, while many universities have sexual violence policies that invoke feminist terms such as "intersectionality," in practice, intersectionality is rarely operationalized.[24] While effectively recognizing that those who experience sexual violence frequently experience numerous forms of marginalization, Canadian campus sexual violence policies employ what Emily Colpitts calls "ornamental intersectionality."[25] The university capitalizes on the language popularized by feminist activism without addressing the root cause of structural injustice for students who face numerous and intersecting forms of marginalization.[26]

There have been significant empirical challenges to these newly enacted "intersectional" sexual violence policies. For instance, legal scholar Karen Busby researched policies adopted as of June 30, 2018. She found that the strict confidentiality clauses embedded in most reporting mechanisms and the lack of publicly available data on reports and responses made it impossible to assess the effectiveness of such policies or how intersectionality actually works within complaint mechanisms.[27]

Despite new policies, programming, and sexual violence offices, universities do not meaningfully protect silence breakers from retaliation. Instead, university complaint processes can unintentionally aid abusive men's retaliation efforts to punish silence breakers. The complaints process cannot decipher between legitimate and frivolous complaints; it has a duty to treat all complaints as serious. As a result, it creates a false equivalency between complaints about sexual violence and retaliatory complaints from those who engage in such behaviour. This false equivalency ultimately upholds unequal power dynamics and fails to protect silence breakers from the weaponization of complaint mechanisms. Allegations of sexual violence disappear as the focus shifts to silence breakers and the harm their complaints have caused the university and the men's reputations. University decision makers first and foremost seek to protect the reputation of the institution; the silence breaker is regarded as disposable.[28] They are forced to drop out of school or resign from their role because of a poisoned campus environment.

The Neoliberal Campus

The university response (or lack thereof) to sexual violence must be situated within a broader social and political context. The university's culture and hierarchies are unique and include power dynamics exacerbated by a shift toward corporate logics in the 1980s.[29] Postsecondary education is viewed as a commodity for economic growth and the "self-betterment" of students, who are consumers.[30] The neoliberal shift to the university as a corporation means that moral obligations are subordinated to economic concerns.[31] Sexual violence prevention and response must be situated within the neoliberalization of postsecondary institutions that prioritize branding through strategic reputational and risk management.[32]

Chapter 2 introduced the importance of individual reputation. A similar analysis can be applied to neoliberal organizations such as universities that are invested in reputational management. Within this logic, firing a university professor for sexual violence may benefit student safety, but the university's reputation is the primary consideration. When the university terminates an employee for sexual violence, their departure often happens quietly to the benefit of the institution and the employee. Frequently, professors leave quietly with no trace that the individual was ever at the university in the first place.[33]

But this practice creates two problems. First, it allows the institution to "pass the harasser" to another institution, which will likely be unaware of the complaints.[34] Second, the problem of sexual violence is reduced to an individual issue with a simple fix – get rid of the "bad apples."[35] The institution can use the termination of an employee strategically to demonstrate that the problem of sexual violence has been solved even as it fails to account for or address the structural issues that allowed it to occur in the first place.[36]

To be clear, while universities will terminate contracts to advance their interests, my research and experience as an antiviolence activist show that the individual who reported sexual violence is more likely to be forced out of their campus community. When a complaint of sexual violence is received, a risk and reputational assessment occurs. The focus is not necessarily on the safety of students but rather on the potential economic consequences, especially if the perpetrator is a well-regarded academic who brings in large research grants. One campus sexual violence worker I interviewed shared that university lawyers often cite the threat of legal action as the primary reason the university cannot act. Lawyers rarely cite the possibility that those who have been harmed will take legal action against the university's failure to act.

I interviewed Canadian antiviolence educator and activist Julie S. Lalonde after she shared on Twitter that she'd been threatened by a university president with a defamation lawsuit because of her advocacy for a campus sexual assault centre. She had just begun her master's degree when a woman was sexually and physically assaulted on campus. From news reports, Lalonde realized the campus did not have adequate support services for campus community members. Lalonde and a friend started to advocate for a sexual violence centre. She felt it would be a quick fix and the university would be eager to make changes to better meet the needs of students. To her surprise, the university was resistant to funding a sexual assault centre. Instead, it focused on the securitization of the campus through a safety audit of its physical environment.[37]

Lalonde organized a series of protests to draw attention to the lack of adequate services. After years of organizing, the president finally agreed to meet with Lalonde. The intimidation tactics began as soon as Lalonde entered her office: "We showed up and [the university president] literally had placed a dictionary in the middle of the table ... No 'hi.' No nothing. No shaking of my hand, just sat down and said, direct quote, 'Pick up the dictionary and read me the definition of libel.'" During the two-hour meeting, the president expressed numerous times that she felt Lalonde's activism was hurting her reputation and that Lalonde should be more careful about the language she used to discuss the university in the media. Lalonde left the meeting with little "proof" of what had occurred, aside from what the person she'd brought with her had witnessed.

Lalonde reflected, "I was, like, oh my God, I'm going to get sued. I'm going to get sued." She was twenty-two years old, from a working-class family, and the first person in her family to go to university. There was a clear power imbalance between her and the university president. Lalonde was warned by others, often with the best of intentions, that if her activism continued, she would likely lose her funding and the university would do anything to ensure she did not finish her degree. She feared being sued and dragged through the legal system by a massive institution with plenty of resources at its disposal. As Sara Ahmed notes, "A method for stopping a complaint is to make it unaffordable."[38] Despite the potential cost, Lalonde felt that the need for a sexual assault centre on campus outweighed what little she had to lose.

Years later, the university opened a sexual assault centre. The history of administrative resistance and outright hostility toward the centre has been lost. Instead, the university administration uses its existence strategically to demonstrate how seriously it takes sexual violence, as an example of its commitment to gender equity on campus.[39] Lalonde's experience is also an explicit example of how the concept of reputation extends beyond the individual to organizations.

Faculty: Missing from the Conversation

I interviewed four faculty members – three females and one male – who were vocal about addressing sexual violence on campus and in turn were sued or threatened with legal action. In addition to the civil legal suits, they experienced other forms of retaliation as well, retaliation that had a significant impact on their professional lives and in turn negatively affected their emotional well-being. While the context of each case differed, the results were the same: a lack of institutional support, institutional retaliation, and reputational damage, even though their universities insisted they took instances of sexual violence seriously.

One of the silence breakers, Gina, was up for tenure. Her department was deeply intertwined with its associated industry outside of academia. At the time, the industry had come under widespread public scrutiny for covering up years of sexual violence disclosures and reports. Gina supported several women who had vocalized their own experiences in national media to highlight the normalization and prevalence of sexual violence within the industry and identify high-profile men known for repeated abusive behaviour. Gina was inspired to support these women because she had been in an abusive relationship with one of the men identified, though she did not publicly identify herself as someone who had experienced abuse by this man.

While much of her activism was done outside of the university, her faculty position was threatened because she supported the women who came forward. She had a falling out with one of her long-time mentors, a highly respected public figure within her industry who publicly supported one of the accused. Gina questioned why her mentor would support these men. In return, her mentor sent her a cease-and-desist letter threatening legal action if she continued with her advocacy efforts. In addition, two of the senior male faculty members in her department, neither of whom had been accused of sexual violence, reported her to the dean and the human rights and equity office, complaining that she "was a danger to them in the era of #MeToo and claiming that they were terrified for themselves." They suggested she "could put them on a list [of abusive men] at any minute and could ruin them with one word."

Gina spoke about the power dynamics between her and her colleagues:

You can lose your job for formal complaints. This was during my tenure review. Two senior tenured professors come at me – and they extract a bunch of promises from me that I won't speak out about [accused name] or about them. Of course, I'll promise anything. I am in my tenure review. If they go forward with a formal complaint, it will go to the provost at the same time as my tenure file, potentially ruining my career. In this climate, if you lose a job – there is no guarantee you are getting another one.

The investigators from the human rights and equity office took a gruelling eight months to find that the allegations of workplace harassment against Gina were unfounded.

Gina's career suffered as a result of the retaliation. She was initially denied tenure, despite having an impressive professional record, forcing her to engage in additional legal action – initiating what would eventually be a successful grievance to reverse the tenure decision. Despite this formal success, Gina continues to face informal consequences. She's stuck in a hostile workplace where it is clear she is not wanted. For example, the retaliating professors demanded she stop attending conferences where they would be in attendance:

> I was deeply depressed. I was suicidally depressed. I upped my meds. I laid in bed. I would get up to take care of the kids. They would go to school, and I would go back to bed. They come home. I would cook for them and go back to bed. There were other times when I couldn't sleep at all. I would be up all night. Just grinding in my head. There aren't even real thoughts. This happened and this happened. How could you do this? How could you think this? I clawed my skin to shreds. I just started scratching and scratching. Yeah. I am pulling out of it now. I am really not ever in public. I have panic attacks about going to work. I've kind of arranged it so I am in and out. I don't see anybody. It's terrible. Tenure now feels like a twenty-year sentence. This simmer of doubt exists around me.

The response to Gina's role as an active bystander of ongoing systemic violence in her professional community had such a serious impact on her professional and personal life that she contemplated suicide.

While Gina was especially vulnerable to intimidation due to her probationary employment status, seniority is no protection from such abuses. Charlene's story is a case in point. A full professor, Charlene was investigated for two disciplinary actions after she supported numerous students who were sexually assaulted and harassed by a tenure-track faculty member in her department. The professor accused of sexual violence filed an internal harassment complaint and an additional internal complaint against Charlene and other colleagues who supported the students. The additional internal complaint requested that the university remove Charlene and one of the other professors from the accused's tenure committee. The university complied.

Charlene elaborated on the consequences of this decision, both for her reputation as a professor and for the department:

> So, they removed us. So, we were actually "punished" on the basis of his complaint against us, effectively removing all of the women from his department from [his] consideration for tenure, including the one woman in his field who would actually be able to evaluate his field. So, by removing us, there were no women from his department on his tenure committee. So, he was being evaluated for tenure in a committee of only men after being accused of sexual harassment. The university added women to his committee, just random women in the university who knew nothing about his field.

Eventually, Charlene and her colleagues were cleared of the allegations that they had harassed her colleague, but she was unable to clear her name publicly as the university deemed the investigators' report confidential. Charlene faced reputational damage because of the investigation into *her* conduct: "It's real reputational damage to be accused of harassment. Even if it's, like, a bluntly ludicrous claim. There are people who will believe it. Universities are super conservative. They are massively dominated by men. A lot of men believe that #MeToo is an exaggerated thing in my world. So, you know, it's not fun."

It is important to highlight the reference Charlene makes to the damage her reputation suffered. While the general focus on sexual violence allegations is the reputational damage endured by men, women also experience reputational damage for their roles as silence breakers. As mentioned, 72 percent of those requesting legal assistance from TIME'S UP Legal Defense Fund experienced retaliation; 15 percent reported that they had been slandered or had their reputation damaged by the perpetrator or their employer.[40]

Like Gina and Charlene, Ali, a university professor introduced in Chapter 1, was also subjected to multiple workplace complaints. The first was made under his university's harassment and discrimination policy. Since the faculty member was unable to prove the allegations, the investigator recommended that the provost dismiss the claim. Then, the professor filed another harassment complaint, claiming Ali's conduct had been in breach of the university's human resources policy. Ali was required to meet with two senior university administrators to discuss the allegations. The administrators encouraged Ali to apologize to his colleague and retract the statements he'd made about the colleague's conduct. After significant back and forth, Ali and the university administrators agreed on the appropriate language to include in a letter to his colleague. The letter would remain in Ali's employee file for five years, though he was told it would not be seen as a disciplinary measure.

Several months later, Ali and two of his colleagues were subjected to yet another complaint when the man accused of sexual violence filed a harassment complaint with the provincial labour tribunal. As a result, Ali was forced to navigate multiple complaints in addition to a civil suit. Ali's experience demonstrates the sheer number of institutional mechanisms available for complaints, and how abusive men can continue to retaliate – after one investigation or tribunal is complete, another begins. These attempts to frame the silence breaker as the actual offender are intended to bully silence breakers back into silence.[41]

For the most part, faculty reported receiving minimal support from their institutions. This is most clear in the case of Julie Macfarlane, who was forced to take the Canadian Universities Reciprocal Insurance Exchange (CURIE) to court after it refused to pay for her lawyer after she was sued for defamation by a former colleague.[42] When Macfarlane sought to defend herself against the lawsuit, she was told that CURIE would not cover her costs as her activities had occurred outside of her professional duties:

> I feel like [the university administrators] just threw me under the bus here. They know that everything I said is true. They know that when a professor in another institution reaches out to a professor and says, "What can you tell me about this person," that we provide informal references in the course of our employment all the time. In this case, it seems to me there was a moral imperative. But, unfortunately, of course, I was the only person who felt that.

CURIE's decision forced Macfarlane into another legal battle. She brought a motion to the Ontario Superior Court to compel CURIE to defend her in the lawsuit, arguing that she was in fact acting within her employment responsibilities. Ultimately, the court decided that CURIE had a duty to defend Macfarlane since she had identified herself as a university professor, used her university email address to contact the new employer, and made statements about E.C.'s conduct during employment at the university. The Superior Court ruled that the nondisclosure agreement did not prohibit Macfarlane from providing a reference to another university and that she was acting within the scope of her duties as a professor by providing a reference. In turn, CURIE had a duty to defend Macfarlane.

Despite the legal victory against CURIE, the defamation proceedings in Trinidad proceeded, and the trial judge ultimately sided with E.C., ordering Macfarlane to pay him approximately $1 million and both parties to stop speaking publicly about the case.[43] To date, there is no evidence to suggest that the plaintiff has attempted to have the order enforced by a Canadian court.

In 2019, I interviewed Julie Macfarlane about this experience. Macfarlane is in a unique location: she is a law professor with decades of experience as an esteemed mediator. Even with these advantages, Macfarlane experienced significant emotional distress and numerous professional challenges because of the lawsuit. Like others, Macfarlane experienced a poisoned work environment following the lawsuit. She talked at length about the lack of institutional support she received from her union, the university administration, and her colleagues. She felt betrayed by the university, because, under the guise of confidentiality, it withheld documents that could have assisted her in fighting the lawsuit.[44] The institutional betrayal and toxic work environment led Macfarlane to resign from her position. She initiated a lawsuit against the University of Windsor for its refusal to provide the plaintiff's termination documents, which could have helped her fight the defamation allegations by proving the reference she provided was true.[45]

Macfarlane's and Charlene's narratives demonstrate that even when faculty members are in senior roles within the academic hierarchy and occupy positions of privilege, they can still face serious reputational damage for taking action to address sexual violence on campus and supporting their students. All four professors – Julie Macfarlane, Charlene, Gina, and Ali – were investigated by their universities. They were subjected to multiple complaints, both within the university and through labour boards. They faced other forms of retaliation – for example, Gina was initially denied tenure while Charlene was removed from a tenure committee. The numerous retaliations significantly impacted their lives on campus and caused reputational damage. Some shared that their colleagues started to distance themselves from them, resulting in social isolation, which led to depression and suicidal ideation.

Given how grave the consequences are for professors, there is concern that they, or others, will be hesitant to support student complaints in the future. Yet, when I asked the professors if they would continue to support survivors of sexual violence, they all enthusiastically said they would. Charlene said the experience taught her how to navigate institutional policies and investigative mechanisms. She wished she had done more:

> The lawsuit taught me a little bit about how to do stuff, you know, the things to avoid and mistakes that maybe we made, like, how to go forward. But, for me, it wouldn't deter me from doing the same thing again. Honestly, I would have done more. I would do more. If I had the same situation again, I would do more ... Because I just didn't know how to do stuff, and now that I've seen a whole scenario play out that was pretty ugly, [it] makes me realize it's doable. You can do it. You just have to be smart about it.

Confirming that he would do more, Ali also recognized that his own experiences as a bystander and supporter, troubling as they were, were still less traumatic than that of someone who has experienced sexual violence:

> What a third-party "whistleblower" goes through in a legal suit is nothing in comparison to what happens to a survivor who is sued for speaking out. With support, I was able to feel good about the stand that I had taken. What made me feel even better was having opportunities to let the [university] administration know that I thought their attempts to establish a sexual misconduct policy fell short, and to support students

agitating for tougher rules. You must not allow such a lawsuit to make you feel afraid, or silence you forever.

Julie Macfarlane expressed similar sentiments:

> There is nothing that I have done that I regret here. There's an absolute moral obligation. I'm sure in the last five and half years, which is what it is since I found out he was suing me, I'm sure I could look back and say, Maybe I shouldn't have done that, and maybe I could have framed that differently. But, basically, I think I've made the right move, in the right way, at the right time. I've always been transparent and honest about it. I've always ... my main focus here is the students, and the safety of the students. That's my obligation, and that's just my obligation. It's what I consider to be my life work. So, there's nothing I regret about this, but it's absolutely extraordinary how it brings it down on our heads in a way that I think it's difficult for people to understand.

These sentiments are encouraging. Perhaps recognizing the broader chilling effects of retaliatory actions, these professors were willing to draw on their relative institutional power to subvert them. University administrators should support this approach – specifically, if administrators want to continue encouraging staff and faculty to be active bystanders, they must also be prepared to protect silence breakers from retaliation. In the current institutional structure, the university has an obligation to investigate complaints, even if the institution knows the reports lack merit – a legal requirement that is well-intentioned, but which can be, and is, abused by abusive men.

The silence breakers' narratives reveal a clear contradiction between what is said to be happening and what is actually happening on campus. On one hand, universities are engaging in public campaigns to prevent and respond to campus sexual violence and creating sexual violence policies and offices. These actions create the illusion that the campus is a space where sexual violence is treated seriously and those who report or disclose it are supported. Postsecondary institutions across the country have responsibilized individuals on campus to become "active bystanders" while simultaneously shifting the responsibility to take concrete action to provide protection or support for silence breakers. Bystanders can face significant consequences and reputational harm when they attempt to use their privilege to address sexual violence. Gina was initially denied tenure and had to file a legal grievance, and Charlene was removed from a tenure committee at the request of the man accused of sexual violence.

These faculty members' experiences demonstrate *how* DARVO (deny, attack, and reverse victim and offender) can operate in postsecondary institutions. By initiating institutional complaints against faculty who have raised concerns about their behaviour, men accused of sexual violence can shift the focus away from the allegations made against them and transform themselves into victims of harassment and unprofessionalism. Their complaints not only centre their own victimization, but they also tie up those who call them out for their misbehaviour in time-consuming and emotionally draining legal and quasi-legal processes. While each of the professors caught up in these complaint processes were ultimately vindicated, the process took years to resolve and resulted in long-term consequences – most notably, a poisoned work environment. Given the significant consequences borne by silence breakers facing legal action, there have been considerable discussions about potential legislative remedies to protect Canadians from retaliatory lawsuits.

5

Is Anti-SLAPP Legislation the Answer?

The term "strategic lawsuits against public participation" (SLAPP) was coined by Penelope Canan and George Pring in the 1980s.[1] SLAPPs are defined as the threat or initiation of litigation that stifles discussion on matters of public interest.[2] The Supreme Court of Canada describes SLAPPs as

> initiated by plaintiffs who engage the court process and use litigation not as a direct tool to vindicate a *bona fide* claim, but as an indirect tool to limit the expression of others. In a SLAPP, the claim is merely a façade for the plaintiff, who is in fact manipulating the judicial system in order to limit the effectiveness of the opposing party's speech and deter that party, or other potential interested parties, from participating in public affairs.[3]

SLAPPs often rely on a range of torts, including but not limited to defamation, tortious interference with contract or business relations, or, in cases of reports to the police, malicious prosecution.[4] A range of activities can result in a SLAPP, including writing a letter to the editor, circulating petitions, contacting a public official, reporting the misconduct of a police officer or teacher to a professional board, speaking at a public meeting, making a submission to city council, reporting unlawful activities, and media interviews.[5] Quebec, Ontario, and British Columbia recognize the consequences of SLAPPs and have introduced legislation to protect citizens from lawsuits intended to stifle expression on matters of public interest.

This chapter examines whether the anti-SLAPP legislation in BC and Ontario is a viable legal remedy for the early dismissal of lawsuits against silence breakers.[6]

SLAPPs as a Feminist Issue

Until recently, SLAPPs were understood by scholars and in public discourse as lawsuits initiated by wealthy corporations or individuals against a genderless defendant involved in some form of political activism, such as environmental activism or protesting property development. Following the passage of anti-SLAPP legislation in Canada and the rise of #MeToo, lawyers and antiviolence organizations argued that lawsuits initiated by men accused of sexual violence ought to be recognized as SLAPPs because of their ability to chill sexual violence discourse, including reporting to institutional bodies.[7]

These lawsuits diverge from the SLAPPs discussed in the literature in that they often occur between two citizens. While plaintiffs usually have some degree of privilege, as they need financial resources to pursue litigation, these men are not always wealthy or powerful. There is also a gendered component in that the plaintiff is most often a cis man, and the defendant most often identifies as a woman. Additional power dynamics come into play given that the defendant is forced into an adversarial process with the man they accused of violence. The consequences of a lawsuit for the individual are immense, as discussed in Chapter 3. Such lawsuits not only impact those who are sued or threatened with a lawsuit, but they also silence public conversations about sexual violence. For this reason, lawsuits targeting those who speak or report sexual violence should be recognized as SLAPPs that require a gendered analysis of power between the two parties.

When Ontario was in the development stages of its anti-SLAPP legislation, Marilou McPhedran and Patricia Freeman Marshall, both long-time antiviolence advocates, testified at Queen's Park about the systemic negative impact lawsuits can have on addressing sexual violence meaningfully.[8] A decade after the Ontario Medical Association had initiated a defamation lawsuit against her (see Chapter 1), McPhedran testified that the lawsuit had stopped her advocacy efforts and those of other advocates working on the issue of patient abuse by medically regulated health professionals. The consequences of the lawsuit were widespread. McPhedran emphasized that the five minutes allotted to her to testify could not "convey the extent of the silencing effect that this SLAPP suit had on awareness and accountability for the sexual abuse of patients, estimated in 2000 to be affecting over 200,000 patients of regulated health professionals in Ontario."[9] Freeman Marshall, who was not a named party on the lawsuit, spoke about the chilling effect the lawsuit had on her:

> I came to appreciate, from that, that my own careful responses would be no defence against such a use of the current law, and with my own health compromised by decades of heartbreaking work with thousands of abuse survivors, I decided to stop speaking publicly. I cut out my advocate's tongue. The libel chill that is invisible to most does have faces and one of them is mine. It's been agonizingly real for me as I know it has been for others.[10]

As this testimony shows, SLAPPs have the power to push matters of sexual violence out of the public consciousness.

Introducing Anti-SLAPP Legislation

In 2015, Ontario passed the *Protection of Public Participation Act* (2015), which amended the *Courts of Justice Act* to include sections 137.1–137.5, "Prevention of Proceedings that Limit Expression on Matters of Public Interest (Gag Proceedings)." Section 137.1(1) states that the purpose of the sections is:

(a) To encourage individuals to express themselves on matters of public interest;
(b) To promote broad participation in debates on matters of public interest;
(c) To discourage the use of litigation as a means of unduly limiting expression on matters of public interest; and
(d) To reduce the risk that participation by the public in debates on matters of public interest will be hampered by fear of legal action.[11]

The legislation's explicit intent is to protect freedom of expression relating to matters of public interest. To allow for broad interpretation, the legislation does not narrowly define what constitutes public interest. As a procedural matter, section 137.1(3) of the *Courts of Justice Act* allows the defendant to ask the courts to dismiss a claim against them on the basis that the claim unduly limits expression on a matter of public interest. In 2019, BC passed nearly identical legislation under the *Protection of Public Participation Act*.[12]

In 2020, the Supreme Court of Canada released two decisions clarifying section 137.[13] Courts are required to undertake a three-step test to decide whether a lawsuit should be dismissed. The first step is the threshold requirement. This step requires the defendant to establish that the proceeding arises from an expression that relates to a matter of public interest.[14] The Supreme Court noted that in the legislation the term "public interest" is

> preceded by the modifier *"a matter of."* This is important, as it is not legally relevant whether the expression is desirable or deleterious, valuable, or vexatious, or whether it helps or hampers the public interest – there is no qualitative assessment of the expression at this stage. *The question is only whether the expression pertains to any matter of public interest, defined broadly.*[15]

The second step is the merits-based hurdle. There are two stages in this step. The plaintiff must demonstrate that the claim has substantial merit. In a defamation claim, the plaintiff is not required to prove the extent of the reputational damage, only that a "realistic threat that the statement, in its full context, would reduce a reasonable person's opinion of that plaintiff."[16] Next, the plaintiff must demonstrate that the defendant(s) have no valid defences. The defendant is then required to raise all the defences that will be relied upon. (See Chapter 2 for a full description of the available defences in defamation claims.) It is then up to the plaintiff to demonstrate that none of the defences will have any prospect of success.

The final step is the public-interest hurdle, which the Supreme Court defines as the "crux" of anti-SLAPP legislation.[17] In this step, the motion judge must assess "how allowing individuals or organizations to vindicate their rights through a lawsuit, a fundamental value in its own right in a democracy, affects in turn, freedom of expression and its corresponding influence on discourse and participation in a pluralistic democracy."[18] The plaintiff must demonstrate that the harm they have suffered because of the expression is "sufficiently serious that the public interest in permitting the proceeding to continue outweighs the public interest in protecting that expression."[19] The court must then weigh the public interest of the expression and its harm to the plaintiff. While the Supreme Court reaffirmed that freedom of expression is the "cornerstone of pluralistic democracy," it also emphasized "that freedom of expression is not absolute" and that the law of defamation must protect a person from an unjustified assault.[20]

When the legislation was before the Supreme Court in 2019, two antiviolence organizations intervened to argue that the legislation must give special consideration to speech about gendered violence, which they argued included formal reports to institutional bodies such as the police. One of the antiviolence groups, the BC Coalition, argued that the courts must recognize the "superordinate public interest in promoting and facilitating the reporting, disclosure, and discussion of gender-based violence such that it will rarely be outweighed by the purported harm to the plaintiff."[21] Furthermore, the BC Coalition argued that people who experience sexual violence need to have confidence that "the courts will apply a test that does not, in the name of formal equality, prefer the plaintiff over the defendant-survivor."[22] From its perspective, men's reputational rehabilitation "must give way to the greater societal interest in ensuring justice for survivors of gender-based violence, and dismantling rather than entrenching impunity for perpetrators."[23]

The Barbra Schlifer Commemorative Clinic, a Toronto-based legal clinic for women who have experienced violence, echoed these sentiments and encouraged the Supreme Court to provide guidance to the lower courts regarding disclosures of sexual violence being matters of public interest that ought to be captured by the legislation.[24] Unsurprisingly, the decision did not address the unique contexts of lawsuits filed by men accused of sexual violence. The interventions of the two groups, however, did raise important points about the need to protect disclosures and reports of gendered violence from retaliatory lawsuits, often involving claims of defamation or malicious prosecution.

SLAPPs and Gendered Violence

Since the introduction of anti-SLAPP legislation in Ontario and British Columbia, there have been a handful of reported decisions where defendants being sued for reporting or disclosing sexual violence have applied to the court to have the lawsuit against them dismissed on the grounds that the lawsuit unduly limits free expression on matters of public interest. The case law reveals four distinct types of communication about gendered violence. Two of them – social media allegations about a specific perpetrator and traditional media reporting on a case of gendered violence – are in the realm of traditional and social media.[25] The third category is speech by the defendant about the gendered violence, including formal reporting or disclosure.[26] The fourth category is lawsuits initiated against bystanders who supported the individual who reported or disclosed.[27]

Here, I examine seven anti-SLAPP decisions to provide insight into how future motions involving gendered violence may be protected by anti-SLAPP legislation. *Rizvee v Newman* (2017) involved Azim Rizvee, a candidate in the 2015 Ontario election. Stacey Newman, a Milton woman, wrote in a series of blog posts and on her personal social media account that Rizvee had bullied and harassed her.[28] Newman reported the harassment to the police and initiated the proceedings for a peace bond under section 810 of the Criminal Code, on the basis that she had reasonable grounds to fear that he would cause her personal injury or damage her property.[29] In March 2016, the peace bond proceedings were addressed in court. The Crown went on the record, warning Rizvee that Newman was fearful of him and "does not with [sic] you to ever touch her, speak directly to her, or enter into her personal space going forward from today. So, hopefully, that is clearly understood."[30] The Crown acknowledged that Newman was fearful of Rizvee but ultimately asked for the peace bond application to be withdrawn. From the decision, it is unclear why the Crown opted to withdraw the application or what role Newman may have played in this decision.[31]

The motion judge dismissed the defamation lawsuit, stating that Newman's speech was protected under section 137.1, but the judge allowed the malicious prosecution lawsuit to proceed. They reasoned that because Newman sought a peace bond by making a report to a justice of the peace, the peace bond was not a matter of public interest: "This was a statement provided by Ms. Newman relating to a private matter, namely whether the state would intervene to restrict Mr. Rizvee's actions in relation to her."[32] The motion judge failed to recognize gendered violence as a matter of public interest, redefining it instead as a private, interpersonal matter between two citizens. This remarkable twist in logic happened despite growing judicial and societal acceptance that gendered violence is a matter of public policy that needs to be addressed by the state. Although the outcome was eventually favourable for Newman (Rizvee eventually abandoned the lawsuit), the legal decision demonstrates the reluctance of the court to protect silence breakers seeking legal protection from institutional bodies.[33]

In *Ng v C.G.* (2020), a case also involving a claim of malicious prosecution, the lawsuit was dismissed entirely. In 2013, C.G., the seventeen-year-old defendant, told her guidance counsellor that she had been sexually assaulted by her former piano teacher. C.G. reported that the sexual assaults occurred between 2009 and 2012. Following C.G.'s disclosure, she insisted she did not want to report the assaults to the police. The guidance counsellor decided that he was under a duty to report the matter and did so without consulting C.G. After the police were called, C.G. decided to make a formal statement. Ng was charged with sexual assault and sexual interference. Following C.G.'s report, the detective revealed that Ng had been charged in 2007 for a sexual assault that involved similar conduct, but the charges were dropped. In C.G.'s case, the preliminary inquiry led to a criminal trial. On the eve of the trial, C.G. requested that the Crown stay the charges against Ng. In turn, Ng initiated a civil action against C.G. for malicious prosecution.[34] C.G. argued that the lawsuit was a SLAPP.

The court emphasized the strong public interest in "persons who believe they have been sexually assaulted, making reports to the police. This is particularly the case when the person alleged to have committed the sexual assault is a teacher who continues to be in close contact with young people."[35] Further, the court questioned Ng's motives in bringing a questionable case against a young university student with little or no expectation of recovering the $1 million in damages he claimed. Rather, the court stated that the action may have been initiated to punish C.G. while also sending a "message to other students who may consider making a report against Ng."[36] Ultimately, the court concluded that the harm in preventing the claim to proceed did not outweigh the public interest. The action against C.G. was dismissed.

Mazhar v Farooqi (2020) is an example of litigation that followed a written report of gendered harassment to a not-for-profit organization, where both parties volunteered.[37] The defendant made a complaint to leadership that the plaintiff had been harassing her for approximately four years. She decided to report Mazhar's conduct after he sent her an email that she found particularly disturbing. She included Mazhar's email in her complaint. Following the complaint, the director advised Mazhar that he was not to attend an upcoming event that the defendant would be hosting and that his volunteer activities were suspended pending the outcome of an internal investigation. The committee overseeing the investigation decided that there was no reason for Mazhar to discontinue his duties as a volunteer. Mazhar sent the defendant a cease-and-desist letter and demanded that she comply with his terms. The motion judge noted the aggressive nature of the letter. It exaggerated the allegations made against Mazhar, he demanded she cease volunteering with the organization for the next five years, and he demanded that her entire family apologize to him.[38] When she did not comply with the demands outlined in the letter, he commenced a defamation action several months later. The defendant did not file a statement of defence and brought forward an anti-SLAPP motion. The motion judge dismissed the legal action against the defendant.

The anti-SLAPP motion in this case was successful for several reasons. The court noted that the defendant had been careful in the language she used to disclose the allegations to the organization. The court noted that she had a moral and social duty to inform the organization of the conduct of one of their volunteers. The court also took into consideration the fact that the investigation was done privately and not communicated to other members, either by the defendant or the organization. Mazhar was unable to successfully demonstrate that the reputational harm of the statement outweighed the need to protect the defendant's expression on a matter of public interest.

The decisions in *Rizvee*, *Ng*, and *Mazhar* demonstrate that anti-SLAPP legislation has the potential to protect people who make formal reports of gendered violence to institutional bodies.

In *Galloway v A.B.*, Steven Galloway sued A.B. as well as over twenty others, many of whom were sued for public commentary on social media. A.B. made a formal report to UBC that Galloway had sexually assaulted her and disclosed the assault to a close friend and two professors (one was her thesis supervisor and equity officer for the department and the acting chair of the department). Galloway insisted that he was not suing A.B. for making a formal report to the university but rather for the additional statements that she made regarding the report. The motion judge dismissed the defamation claim against A.B. for statements made in 2015; however, the motion judge agreed with Galloway that A.B. had exceeded the scope of qualified privilege under the formal reporting process at the university when she spoke to her thesis supervisor and acting chair of the department and gave them permission to speak to others about the allegations.

At the time of writing, A.B. is appealing the decision because it raises considerable concerns for the protection of those who may disclose or report sexual violence using institutional processes. *Rizvee, Farooqi, and Ng* demonstrate that some defendants have been successful in obtaining orders dismissing the legal action, but *Galloway* reveals that the scope of anti-SLAPP legislation remains uncertain and likely limited.

The cases of *Lyncaster v Metro Vancouver Kink Society* (2019) and *Smith v Nagy* (2021) demonstrate the limitations of anti-SLAPP legislation when social media is used to communicate allegations of sexual violence. In these two cases, the anti-SLAPP motions were dismissed, and the defamation action proceeded. In *Lyncaster*, the plaintiff, Seann Lyncaster, a Burnaby dungeon master who went by the name Lord Braven in the kink community, initiated a defamation action against Metro Vancouver Kink Society (MVKS). In 2018, MVKS posted an open letter addressed to Lyncaster on its social media alleging that several members of the community had come forward with allegations of consent violations against Lyncaster. The letter states that the members asked Lyncaster to participate in a community-based restorative justice process, but he denied the request.[39] The letter also stated that MVKS would no longer recommend his home as being safe for members, rent space for him, advertise his events, or allow him to volunteer or teach at MVKS. Following the publication of the open letter, MVKS hosted a town hall to discuss the allegations.[40] The release of the open letter and the town hall resulted in numerous people coming forward with allegations that Lyncaster had violated their consent.[41]

Lyncaster sued the MVKS's board, alleging that the open letter, town hall meeting, and circulation of meeting minutes had negatively impacted his standing within the kink community, resulting in reduced attendance at events he hosted and preventing him from conducting workshops, which, as a result, led to a loss of income and increased levels of personal stress.[42] Lyncaster sought pecuniary damages and an injunction against MVKS to prevent any additional damage to his reputation. In turn, MVKS attempted to have the case dismissed, arguing that the legal action stifled public speech on matters of public interest.

MVKS was successful at the first stage of the anti-SLAPP test. It demonstrated that the intention of the communication was of public interest, namely, to protect the health and safety of the kink community.[43] At the second step, the motion judge, Justice Mayer, found that the case had substantial merit. Furthermore, the judge decided that Lyncaster had proved that the defence of qualified privilege (which MVKS had pled) could not reasonably succeed at trial. At the weighing stage, Mayer was clear that "not all expressions on matters of public interest serve the values underlying freedom of expression," especially in cases involving allegations of criminal misconduct.[44] Mayer emphasized that he was not satisfied with the justification of the public interest element of the social media post; the Vancouver kink community could have reported the allegations of criminal misconduct to the police.[45] But in the decision, Mayer failed to acknowledge why members of the kink community, specifically those who engage in BDSM, may be apprehensive about reporting to the police.[46] It is entirely possible (and expected) that the police and the courts would diminish their claims of sexual violence by claiming they were simply a natural byproduct of engaging in BDSM or kink.[47] There is a lack of recognition about why some communities may prefer to rely on nonlegal forums, such as the restorative justice process requested of Lyncaster, as opposed to the carceral system. Ultimately, the motion was dismissed, and the lawsuit proceeded.

Smith v Nagy shares many similarities to *Lyncaster*. Zak Smith, who goes by the name Zak Sabbath, is a game creator and adult performer who was married to Amanda Nagy, known as Mandy Morbid, a model and adult film performer. After their marriage ended, Nagy posted a lengthy public Facebook post alleging that during the decade of their relationship, Smith sexually, physically, and emotionally abused her and other women. The post was shared over nine hundred times, received over two hundred comments, and approximately two thousand Facebook users "liked" the post. Within days, Smith was barred from numerous online-gaming communities. In turn, Smith demanded Nagy take down the Facebook post, to which she refused. He served her with a lawsuit.

Nagy initiated a section 137 motion to have the claim dismissed, arguing that the communications should be protected as they relate to a matter of public interest. Smith argued that the matters were private and should not have been shared publicly. While the court ultimately agreed that Nagy's post was a matter of public interest, the justice cautioned that "not every allegation of sexual misconduct by one person against another engages the public interest, even if one or more of them is a public figure."[48] In this case, because Nagy's social media post about the relationship resulted in a broader debate about gendered violence and challenged the couple's public persona of being in a happy polyamorous relationship, the allegations were decidedly a matter of public interest.[49] While Nagy was able to satisfy the first stage of the test, at the next stages, the court decided that Smith's claim had substantial merit and that the harm he suffered outweighed the public interest in protecting Nagy's expression. The motion was dismissed, and the lawsuit remains before the courts.

In both *Lyncaster* and *Smith,* the defendants made social media posts about the plaintiff's behaviour that included allegations of sexual violence. All parties were involved in the kink and broader sex community and were held in high regard in their communities. As a result, the social media posts alleging sexual violence were widely shared and became the topic of widespread community discussion about consent violations and gendered violence more generally. Although the motion decisions may be sound from a legal perspective, they also signal the limitations of anti-SLAPP legislation in cases involving public declarations of violence. Furthermore, the decisions raise questions about how individuals and communities ought to communicate concerns about sexual harm, particularly in cases where the members of the community may be reluctant to rely on the formal legal system for a range of reasons such as involvement in the sex industry or other forms of systemic marginalization. In contrast, section 137 was a successful mechanism in *Mazhar* and *Ng* because the defendants in both cases had made reports in confidence and through official reporting channels.

The final category of anti-SLAPP motions involves journalists who have reported on gendered violence. To date, there has been one successful anti-SLAPP motion following a media publication on domestic violence. In *Bullard v Rogers Media Inc* (2020), the plaintiff, a comedian and radio personality, was charged with several offences, including criminal harassment and harassing communications.[50] Following the preliminary trial, the criminal harassment charges were dropped, and he pled guilty to harassing communications. Since both parties were prominent figures in Toronto media, the charges and subsequent guilty plea received local media attention.

Following the conclusion of the criminal proceedings, journalist Sarah Boesveld wrote a story about the charges that included an interview with the victim. Following the publication of the story, Bullard sued Rogers Media, the executive editor, and Sarah Boesveld for defamation. Bullard did not include the woman he harmed in the lawsuit. In the statement of claim, Bullard identified thirteen defamatory statements in the article. The statements claimed that the woman had feared for her safety to the extent that she moved out of her house. Bullard argued that this had not been substantiated by the courts, as they dismissed the criminal harassment charges.

The defendant's section 137 motion was successful because it was decided that if the lawsuit were to proceed, it would negatively impact expression on a matter of public interest. The motion judge, Justice McKelvey, affirmed the necessity of ensuring that discussions of gendered violence were protected as a matter of public interest. McKelvey wrote that in some circumstances, "permitting the wronged party to seek vindication through litigation comes at too high a cost to freedom of expression."[51] Furthermore, the decision explicitly stated the value of expression about gendered violence: "The value of freedom of expression is high in this case. Gender based abuse is recognized as a serious social problem in our society. It is generally understood that there are systemic barriers to reporting this type of activity. The consequences of gender based harassment are too often severe and the public interest in expression on this topic is high."[52]

Taken together, these cases provide important insight into the potential opportunities and limitations of anti-SLAPP legislation. While the outcomes of the motions were varied, several themes run among them. For one, the lower courts have been clear that gendered and sexualized violence is a matter of public interest. What is of paramount importance is the mode of disclosing or reporting the violence. Defendants who relied on formal reporting mechanisms were more likely to have the lawsuit against them dismissed than defendants who relied on social media.

The Challenges of Anti-SLAPP Legislation

Anti-SLAPP legislation could be a promising option for people sued for making formal reports to the police, their workplace, or a university. But there are numerous barriers. Such motions are incredibly complex, making them expensive and time-consuming and often invasive, particularly the demands of discovery-like document production and cross-examination on affidavit.

In interviews, several lawyers shared that initiating an anti-SLAPP motion is not necessarily a good use of resources and time. One lawyer pointed out that to be successful, the defendant is required to file a motion along with supporting evidence, often an affidavit. The affidavit typically provides context for the circumstances that led to the lawsuit. In the case of sexual violence, this would mean including a detailed narrative of the sexual violence and any formal reports that were made to the police or other institutions, such as a university. The affidavit must also demonstrate the silencing impact of the lawsuit and establish that the communication relates to a matter of public interest. The plaintiff can, in turn, file an affidavit to establish their version of events, argue that the claim has substantial merit, and prove that the reputational harm they experienced outweighs the public interest. Prior to the motion being heard in court, the parties can be cross-examined on their affidavits for up to seven hours in total.[53]

In cases involving allegations of sexual violence, the affidavit and cross-examination are often a concern. One lawyer I interviewed who had represented several women who had initiated anti-SLAPP motions said they can cause significant emotional and psychological distress, including suicidal ideation. Although the cross-examination happens outside a courtroom, is more private in comparison to a public criminal trial, and the silence breaker will likely have legal counsel representing her, she can still be subjected to hostile questions intended to humiliate and shame her.[54] The lawyer I interviewed argued that if the purpose of the anti-SLAPP legislation is to prevent the silencing of speech, it fails each time litigating the motion prevents people from speaking out about sexual violence.

In addition to the affidavit and cross-examination, the plaintiff's counsel may request documents identified in the affidavit, during cross-examination, or that the plaintiff suspects the defendant may have in her possession. As discussed in Chapter 1, men can take advantage of document production by requesting highly personal information about the defendant such as personal correspondence with friends or institutional records.[55] For example, in *Galloway,* the plaintiff requested extensive document production from A.B. and her supporters, including two professors and friends who commented on the case on social media.[56] The defendants objected to the request on the basis that the number of documents requested was excessive and that they were private in nature. The requested documents included all correspondence regarding the disclosure of the sexual assault, a list of every person A.B. talked to about the allegations, a draft civil claim against the university for its handling of the sexual assault report, all correspondence about the sexual assault with specific individuals named by the plaintiff, and any Facebook or Twitter posts regarding an article the defendants wrote about the plaintiff. The plaintiff argued that the privacy rights of the defendants were of secondary importance to defending his reputation.

In July 2019, I attended the two-day court hearing to decide whether the documents should be produced. The plaintiff described the woman who reported the sexual assault as hysterical and argued that her inability to maintain her composure during the cross-examination justified the need for extensive documentation to verify her version of events. His allegation that she was hysterical conformed to the gendered trope that women who disclose sexual violence are mentally unwell.[57]

Ultimately, the court sided with the plaintiff and ordered most of the documents to be produced. The exceptions were her disclosure of the sexual violence to a professor, a list of the people she disclosed to, and communications between A.B. and her legal counsel. The defendants appealed the decision, arguing that privacy concerns outweighed the reputational interests of the plaintiff. The Court of Appeal again sided with the plaintiff. The Court stated that although A.B. had been required to produce highly personal and prejudicial documents, if the lower court had denied the production of these documents, the potential prejudice to the plaintiff's reputational interests would have been greater.[58]

Wanda, one of the silence breakers I interviewed, was in a similar situation when she brought an anti-SLAPP motion. She was required to produce highly personal correspondence, which she tied to the financial resource disparities between the two parties. She initially objected to the document production, and he successfully argued before the court that she had to produce them. As the litigation moved forward, she learned of documents he had in his possession that could assist her in establishing a valid defence. Ultimately, she decided that it would be too expensive to take the matter before the court to have him produce the documents:

> The court decided that the importance of me producing documents was very high because if you don't, the plaintiff will lose. So, fairness says that he should have everything relevant. Otherwise, he is on the back foot. He's at risk. He is at risk of having the litigation being cancelled. So, you can't just wiggle out of document production, but he didn't have to produce anything. You know, there could have been things that would have demonstrated the truth of the allegations. He hasn't been compelled to produce certain documents, and he got away with it, and the cost of going to court to argue it – it just wasn't worth it or wasn't likely to be successful.

She felt the anti-SLAPP motion provided yet another legal avenue for the abusive man to terrorize those who questioned his behaviour.

Wanda expanded on how sexual violence differed from other types of SLAPPs:

> For example, if you are protesting a pipeline, the pipeline takes up space, and there's interactions with the natural world. You can have scientists

who have opinions on that with data ... Sexual violence is a criminal act that includes consent. Consent is a state of mind. And that's not ... that's not anything that can be captured except through testimony. There might possibly be documents that are relevant to it. But often [document production] is just to abuse the person further. The argument is, "I want to see if the person actually talked about the rape." But it's just a way to terrorize someone, to attack their credibility if there is any slight difference in the way a document records a conversation.

To be clear, she was not suggesting that she should not have to produce any documents. Rather, she felt the document production could have been more equitable between the parties. For example, given the financial disparities between herself and the plaintiff, she did not have the same resources to go to court to request documents that she'd learned about during the motion proceedings. In contrast, the plaintiff got a court order requiring her to produce a series of documents, including private conversations and access to her social media accounts, which are private.

I am also not suggesting that the plaintiff should not have access to *any* documents associated with the allegations made about him. The point here is to demonstrate that the production of documents in this early stage can be invasive, replicating abusive power dynamics that are unique to sexual violence cases. Access to financial resources is critical. For instance, many of the plaintiffs in the cases had far more financial resources in comparison to the defendants.

The *Galloway* decision illustrates another issue. Lise Gotell argues that the sheer volume of documentation required to "prove" a woman's credibility marks the emergence of a new iteration of the "ideal victim." Whereas the ideal victim was once defined by her sexual morality, she is now defined by her consistency and rationality.[59] The ideal victim makes the "right" choices in her own self-governance by limiting the people she discloses to. But the so-called ideal number of disclosures has yet to be defined by the courts. Those who cannot demonstrate their ability to "maintain their composure" and psychological stability, as described by the lawyer above, are at risk of losing the protections afforded by privacy rights.[60]

We cannot assume that document production is a neutral or straightforward process. Given that the anti-SLAPP legislation is still relatively new, it is likely too soon to make empirical claims about whether and how often the motion replicates discovery in civil cases more generally. What can be inferred from these cases is the extent to which women who experience sexual violence are required to "prove" their allegations in a space that replicates a criminal sexual assault trial more than in other defamation proceedings.

The other concern about anti-SLAPP motions is their time and cost. The legislation was intended to provide defendants in lawsuits with a mechanism to achieve a dismissal in a timely, cost-effective manner. Defamation scholar Hilary Young raised similar concerns in *Canadian Lawyer*, noting that these motions are "neither quick nor cheap." Young interviewed several lawyers who have litigated SLAPP motions. None were taken on contingency, making them financially risky for defendants.[61] Another lawyer I interviewed shared similar concerns about the cost of bringing forward an anti-SLAPP motion. This lawyer explicitly referenced document production related to counselling records or private communications as an example of the way the anti-SLAPP motion can become costly and time-consuming for both parties.

Wanda's experience of the anti-SLAPP motion is a perfect example of how quickly the cost and time can add up. In total, it took two years from the time she filed the motion for the court to come to a decision. The delay was due to several procedural disputes regarding document production that resulted in court hearings that spanned multiple days. By the time the motion was completed, the motion cost her approximately $80,000 in legal fees, even with a generous discount from her lawyers. In the end, her anti-SLAPP motion was not successful. Although her lawyers encouraged her to appeal the decision, she decided it would be too financially risky to do so and would prolong the matter even longer.

She shared with me that when she first learned of the legislation, she was hopeful because she thought it would be an appropriate mechanism to dismiss the lawsuit against her. In retrospect, she said that knowing what she now knows about the process itself, she would not pursue this avenue. Further, she also cautioned that she wouldn't recommend it to anyone else. She felt she would have been better off just taking the matter to trial.

The existence of anti-SLAPP legislation offers the illusion of a cost-effective and quick way for silence breakers to have lawsuits against them dismissed.

Since the introduction of the legislation, I have heard from women living in provinces without anti-SLAPP legislation that they would be inclined to speak publicly about the sexual violence they experienced if anti-SLAPP protections existed in their province. Such assumptions wrongly assume that anti-SLAPP motions are as straightforward and cost-effective as they were originally intended. Furthermore, the case law from Ontario and BC has demonstrated that there is no guarantee that the courts are willing to dismiss lawsuits regarding allegations of sexual violence on an anti-SLAPP motion.

In this chapter, I have attempted to dispel misinformation about anti-SLAPP legislation. But regardless of whether a motion is successful, litigation is time-consuming and expensive, especially in cases of defamation given the complexity of this area of law. And litigation can be psychologically and emotionally difficult. There is also the potential for document production that may include personal correspondence and other private records. Although document production can occur regardless in the discovery phase, people must be aware of this reality if they plan to rely on anti-SLAPP legislation prior to making public statements about sexual violence. The anti-SLAPP decisions tell us that formal reports will potentially be protected by anti-SLAPP legislation while, unsurprisingly, the courts have opted not to dismiss defamation lawsuits relating to sexual violence disclosures on social media.

Conclusion

This book examines the multilayered consequences of men accused of sexual violence suing silence breakers for defamation. The research was guided by three inquiries: (1) What are the individual and societal consequences of defamation lawsuits against silence breakers? (2) How do these lawsuits push sexual violence discourse from the public sphere and aid in the reprivatization of sexual violence in Canada? (3) Are these lawsuits strategic lawsuits against public participation (SLAPPs) and can anti-SLAPP legislation protect silence breakers from retaliatory lawsuits?[1]

Before I provide a synopsis of my findings, I will address the limitations. The biggest limitation of this study is my fear of being sued for defamation. There were moments I contemplated not publishing this book out of fear of a retaliatory lawsuit. Regardless of how careful I am with my words, many of the men discussed in the chapters of this book are litigious. As a precariously employed academic without any job security, I worry that the consequences of being forced to defend myself in another lawsuit could destroy me, emotionally, financially, and professionally. In this book, I do exactly what I criticize the media for doing: I strategically water down allegations and leave out certain details to protect myself and the silence breakers I interviewed.

I also provide fewer details about how the identity of the silence breakers influenced the legal proceedings than I would have liked. While lawsuits against silence breakers appear to be a growing trend globally, overall, lawsuits of this kind are still relatively rare. Just a few minor details about the lawsuit and the identity of the parties can reveal the identities of the research participants. It is my ethical duty as a researcher to protect research participants from retaliation or other consequences of participating in this study. The unfortunate result is that I have only scraped the surface when it comes to showing how intersecting forms of structural oppression shape silence breakers' experiences of sexual violence and the subsequent retaliation.

The final limitation I wish to address is a systemic one. The data collected on civil legal actions in Canada is limited. Statistics Canada collects data on the number of cases initiated, the number of total active cases, the number of events within the last year (for example, an aggregate number of settlements, the number of lawsuits withdrawn or abandoned, and document filings), and the number of the most common types of civil action.[2] Defamation is not listed as an action for which specific data is collected; instead, "defamation" falls under the broad category "other Tort," making it challenging to assess the frequency of defamation actions even generally.

Few Canadian scholars have studied defamation, and those who have or do tend to be legal researchers interested in reported decisions. Overall, Canadian legal practitioners, scholars, and policymakers would benefit from interdisciplinary research on defamation actions. Our collective knowledge about defamation law in practice in Canada is limited. Even more specifically, as argued throughout this book, we need to continue monitoring the frequency of lawsuits against silence breakers. Research on this subset of defamation lawsuits could be a useful tool for future feminist advocacy and policy considerations.

Key Findings

In the absence of quantitative data about defamation suits against silence breakers, this study offers several important conclusions: (1) a systemic failure to respond to sexual violence makes silence breakers vulnerable to litigation, (2) defamation suits threaten to silence discourse on sexual violence, (3) defamation actions against silence breakers are a form of abusive litigation with significant individual and societal impacts, and (4) defamation suits against silence breakers are a unique form of SLAPP.

Systemic Failure to Respond to Sexual Violence

Many of the silence breakers interviewed relied on formal avenues of reporting. This runs counter to the assumption that defamation lawsuits are typically initiated after women "name and shame" men on social media for some sort of personal benefit. While some of the silence breakers resorted to social media instead of making a formal report, a majority did not. Two of the silence breakers experienced intersecting forms of marginalization, which must be taken into consideration to better understand *why* they opted to use social media.

For example, Catherine only posted about the violence she experienced after the man she reported agreed to a peace bond for causing harm to another person. Although Catherine reported her experience to the police, the police chose not to investigate and instead declared it unfounded. Catherine used social media because the formal avenue to reporting was denied to her. Catherine's experience is similar to that of other women of colour who have been forced to navigate the intersection of sexism and racism when seeking assistance from the police.[3] Access to the formal legal system following a sexual assault is often denied to racialized and Indigenous women.

In other cases, such as *Stuart v Doe*, Jane Doe was sued because she made a formal report to the university, which was acted upon, and Doe was effectively held responsible for the actions the university took. In *Rizvee v Newman*, the Crown refused Stacey Newman a peace bond, which left her vulnerable to being sued for malicious prosecution. In Canada, reports to the police are not necessarily protected from litigation. This makes a silence breaker's use of the criminal legal system a potential liability when a report is used as evidence of her intent to undermine a man's reputation.[4]

This perverse use of formal reporting was most pronounced in Lynn's case. Although it happened in the legal system of another country, the acquittal of the man she accused of rape meant he was able to have her criminally charged with making false allegations as well as initiate a civil legal suit. Notably, the Canadian government did nothing to assist Lynn or intervene in her case, leaving her to suffer the emotional, psychological, and financial costs alone. For these silence breakers, formal reporting mechanisms worked against them. It is, then, not surprising that other research participants made a conscious decision not to report to the police because they did not have confidence in the criminal legal system.

Institutional failure to respond to sexual violence was also evident in the workplace. Four of the silence breakers attempted to report workplace sexual violence and received a range of responses from minimization to outright denial. Laura and Lynn were both fired after they reported. Bonnie Robichaud reported experiencing numerous forms of workplace retaliation, which escalated after she decided to take legal action against her workplace for the sexual harassment and the managerial response to her report. The silence breakers faced varying degrees of backlash, some instigated by the men accused of sexual violence, others by staff members and management who were assisting the accused in orchestrating the silence breakers' punishment.

University faculty members identified similar concerns. They all actively supported individuals who disclosed or reported sexual violence. In addition to taking legal action or threatening the women with a lawsuit, the men accused also initiated complaints of harassment within the university. Although the complaints were eventually dismissed, there were professional consequences for the faculty members – for example, Gina was initially denied tenure, and Charlene was removed from a tenure committee. The threat of legal action against Gina and Charlene caused emotional distress, compounded by lengthy investigations into their conduct. Furthermore, both women noted that they experienced professional reputational damage from being accused and investigated for harassment and that this continued even after they had been cleared of the allegations by a university investigator.

Although universities across the country have funded campaigns and programming aimed at encouraging university community members to become active bystanders, the silence breakers' narratives highlight the lack of structural support within the university for such individuals. Their narratives demonstrate that abusive men will often engage in multiple complaint processes to exhaust silence breakers emotionally and financially. The high cost of litigation contributes to the reprivatization of sexual violence by making silence breakers fearful of reporting and in some cases speaking even generally about sexual violence.

The Disappearance of Sexual Violence Discourse

A defamation lawsuit against a silence breaker does more than reprivatize sexual violence; it pushes the sexual violence into absolute obscurity. As the rulings in cases such as *Whitfield v Whitfield*, *Vanderkooy v Vanderkooy*, *Smith v Nagy*, and *Lyncaster v Metro Vancouver Kink Society* reveal, those who wish to disclose sexual violence are expected to report it to the appropriate authorities.[5] There is an expectation that the sexual violence will not be discussed until the conclusion of an investigation or a court proceeding, and only if there is a finding that the sexual violence did, in fact, occur.

There is little regard for the systemic challenges of reporting sexual violence, the low likelihood of a conviction, and the fact that reporting often entangles the silence breaker in legal or investigative processes that can take years to conclude. In some cases, such as sexual violence allegations involving faculty members where privacy legislation is at play, there is no guarantee that the silence breaker will even be made aware of the outcome of the investigation.[6] While the courts agree that gendered violence is a serious issue, they have also condemned silence breakers for not disclosing their sexual violence the right way. However, the court has yet to provide clear guidance about how many people and who it is acceptable to disclose sexual violence to, or what language silence breakers can use to describe the violence. Regardless, the recent legal decisions make it risky for someone who has experienced sexual violence to disclose sexual violence to anyone in any context.

Once a defamation action is initiated, or even threatened, allegations of sexual violence shift to allegations of false accusations. People become fearful of acknowledging the allegations of sexual violence out of fear of litigation. For these reasons, I argue that lawsuits suppress discourse about sexual violence and must be explicitly regarded as SLAPPs. The SLAPP literature helps contextualize lawsuits against silence breakers as part of a broader political strategy to silence dissent, but it also needs to be viewed through an explicitly gendered lens to grasp the complexities of power that occur within these lawsuits, including an element of abuse that entrenches existing power dynamics between abuser and silence breaker. To date, the courts have failed to grapple with this uniquely gendered power dynamic in attempts to have defamation lawsuits dismissed under the newly enacted anti-SLAPP legislation.

Lawsuits against silence breakers are effective silencing tools for several reasons. The first is practical. Once a lawsuit has been initiated, most lawyers will instruct their clients to refrain from making any statements about the sexual violence specified within the suit. The second reason is that once a woman has been warned about a lawsuit, a risk assessment may force her to reconsider the cost of continuing to speak out. The financial or personal cost of speaking may be so significant that she decides to self-censor to protect herself from a lawsuit or from additional allegations of defamation that can be added to a lawsuit. Finally, some women agreed to a gag order during legal proceedings, which prohibits to varying degrees (depending on what has been negotiated between the parties) what she can say about the sexual violence she endured or her relationship with the plaintiff. The initiation of a lawsuit not only silences the individuals named on the lawsuit, but it also hinders others from speaking about either the lawsuit or the allegations of sexual violence out of fear that they could be added to the lawsuit.

As demonstrated throughout the book, the censorship embedded in a lawsuit, or the decision to self-censor out of fear of being sued, was cited as having negative effects on silence breakers. Silence breakers often refrained from speaking to anyone about what happened to them out of fear of additional litigation. This censorship negatively impacted their healing processes, leading many of the silence breakers to suicidal ideation. But when women are fearful of speaking about sexual violence, even generally, we risk pushing sexual violence out of the public and back into the private sphere. This is especially true in the civil legal system, where legal proceedings take place between two private citizens.

In the public realm, the media experiences libel chill, which deters outlets from publishing stories about sexual violence. Like individuals, media outlets also worry about potential legal action because of the significant cost and time it takes to mount a defence. It's impossible to quantify libel chill, or the extent to which media is reluctant to report on cases of sexual violence; however, my research findings suggest that defamation lawsuits against media outlets have the potential to censor, water down, or even eliminate important discussions about sexual violence. As discussed in Chapter 4, an Ontario lawyer specializing in sexual abuse claims noticed that since the #MeToo Movement, media outlets have become wary of publishing stories without naming the silence breakers, which has resulted in fewer stories about sexual violence being published. Even simply identifying someone as a "survivor" in a news story has been challenged, as in the case of the *Toronto Star*, where allegations of violence were a minor element of a larger story about a boxing gym that offered classes for people who had experienced gendered violence. Taken together, the chilling of individual speech along with media libel chill is silencing discourse on gendered violence.

Lawsuits against Silence Breakers Are Abusive Litigation

Threatening a lawsuit is an extension of an abusive power dynamic. Silence breakers who were threatened became aware that their abusers were monitoring their actions and social media accounts. Men who initiated or threatened lawsuits frequently engaged in numerous complaint processes against the silence breakers and anyone who attempted to hold them accountable. Jennifer Freyd's concept of deny, attack, reverse victim and offender (DARVO) reflects this reality.[7] Freyd acknowledges that innocent people will defend themselves against false allegations, but it is abusive men who retaliate against anyone who raises concerns about their behaviours. Abusive men rely on ad hominem attacks on the silence breaker to recast themselves as the victim and the silence breaker as the offender.[8] In addition to threatening a lawsuit, a number of the men discussed in these pages reported the silence breaker to the police, alleging harassment, or filed a workplace misconduct report, forcing the silence breaker to defend herself in numerous legal and quasi-legal forums.

Defamation law is the perfect legal tool for abusive men looking to exact revenge on those who call them into account for their abusive behaviours. Defamation law exists solely to protect reputation. All a plaintiff needs to do is launch a lawsuit alleging that the words a silence breaker has used are defamatory, and the burden falls on the silence breaker to defend herself. In instances where the words allege sexual violence, a defamation trial is more likely to resemble a sexual assault trial. The silence breaker is required to prove that what she said was true, a feat that is often challenging given the private nature of most sexual violence and the hesitancy of courts to believe women's testimonies of violence. But what happens within the court is usually irrelevant since so few cases ever make it to trial. The underlying issue here is the mere fact that an abusive man can initiate a lawsuit with such ease. It is the lawsuit itself, rather than the court's decision, that inflicts significant harm on silence breakers.

Many of the silence breakers reported experiencing severe physical symptoms that developed following retaliation, and they linked their symptoms to the stress of being sued. The psychological distress was so severe that it led several to thoughts of suicide. I do not regard the disclosure of suicidal ideation as an indicator of individual pathology; rather, I regard contemplating death as a natural response to a brutalizing legal process that forces silence breakers into an ongoing relationship with their abusers. In addition to navigating institutional retaliation, the silence breaker must also manage the physical symptoms and emotional distress caused by the legal action. Overall, lawsuits had a tremendous impact on the silence breakers, often compounding the traumatic aftermath of the sexual violence. For many of the silence breakers, the institutional retaliation was far more traumatic than the sexual violence itself – for that reason, such lawsuits must be regarded as abusive.

Can lawsuits against silence breakers be classified as SLAPPs? To date, much of the academic literature has failed to account for the unique gender dynamics in SLAPPs involving gendered violence; they instead focus on SLAPPs that centre on traditional forms of political engagement such as lobbying government officials or raising environmental concerns about the business practices of large corporations. In the last several years, lawyers across Canada and the United States have identified retaliatory lawsuits against silence breakers as a growing concern.[9] I argue that sexual violence is an issue of public interest and that reports and disclosures of sexual violence are a form of political speech that must be protected. The legislation that currently exists, while seemingly promising when it was first introduced, is limited in its availability to protect silence breakers' speech.

Recommendations

Between conducting this research and being sued, I have identified recommendations for future advocacy to help protect silence breakers from retaliatory lawsuits. Most obviously, the root cause of these lawsuits is sexual violence; therefore, eliminating sexual violence would prevent such lawsuits from occurring in the first place. But criminal law reforms over many decades have done little to improve formal reporting or decrease self-reported experiences of sexual violence.[10] We cannot rely solely on legal reform to eliminate sexual violence, a deeply embedded social problem. For this reason, I am hesitant to make recommendations that rely too much on changes to the law or legal processes, but I do feel there may be some that are worth pursuing. My recommendations to prevent retaliatory lawsuits fall within three broad categories: broadening the scope of advocacy efforts, education, and legal reform.

The first recommendation is broadening the scope of advocacy efforts to address retaliatory lawsuits that include bystanders and supporters. Advocates who address the issue of retaliatory lawsuits in the courts or media focus on protecting the individual who experienced sexual violence. I argue that this approach is far too narrow. Retaliatory lawsuits tend to target more than the individual who reports or discloses sexual violence; they also target individuals who provide public commentary on the systemic nature of sexual violence, faculty members who support students, and journalists who write about allegations of sexual violence. It is well-established that bystanders are incredibly important in ending sexual violence.[11] Therefore, we must protect them.

The next recommendation is improving education about sexual violence. This recommendation is two-fold. First, one of the major challenges the silence breakers noted was legal counsel who did not understand the power dynamics of sexual violence. One example is the failure to recognize the unique harms that gag orders can have on people who experience sexual violence. While a gag order may be standard practice in settlement negotiations, lawyers need to understand the potential consequences in cases of sexual violence and, if necessary, negotiate a settlement that allows the defendant some latitude to speak about what happened to her.

We need better education and programs for those who work in the antiviolence sector and those who are considering reporting or disclosing sexual violence. These people require knowledge of defamation law and an understanding that making a formal report of sexual violence does not protect the individual from a lawsuit. Similarly, bystanders should be included in these programs, as they would likely benefit from legal information to protect themselves from a lawsuit by an accused party. Even though a vast majority of people who experience sexual violence will not be sued for reporting or disclosing it, women often message me to inquire about the likelihood of being sued before they decide to make a report. The limitation of this recommendation is that these programs won't offer legal representation, which is what is most needed once a lawsuit has been initiated. Thus, robust legal assistance needs to be paired with remedies focused on reducing the scenarios that allow abusive men to sue.

The next recommendation is that advocates and activists who seek remedies outside of the legal system critically examine how such processes will legally protect silence breakers. Rightfully so, there have been many critiques of carceral feminism and the reliance on the state to respond to gendered violence.[12] In theory, transformative justice and restorative justice in response to sexual violence appeal to many people who are critical of carceral feminism and expanding the power of the state, which often results in the overcriminalization of racialized men and women. Several research participants, for political reasons, made the conscious decision not to engage with the criminal legal system after experiencing sexual violence. In turn, they were sued by the men who abused them. How can we protect these women?

The final recommendation is for legal reform to reduce the number of lawsuits initiated following a formal report of sexual violence. While I have serious concerns about the law's potential to provide justice or protect people from sexual violence, there are potential remedies that could help those who are sued for reporting or disclosing. While anti-SLAPP legislation initially provided antiviolence advocates with hope that retaliatory lawsuits would be dismissed, recent legal decisions in Ontario and British Columbia suggest that only selected motions will be successful, typically those that include formal reports and adherence to the expectations of the "good victim" archetype. Furthermore, the anti-SLAPP motion often requires broad document disclosures that resemble a discovery. Finally, anti-SLAPP legislation is, by nature, political and, depending on political interests, could be repealed.[13]

One potential remedy that could help protect people who report or disclose sexual violence is to expand the legal defence of absolute privilege to include formal reports of sexual violence, such as those made to the police. Absolute privilege is typically applied to statements made in judicial and quasi-judicial spaces.[14] The English courts have ruled that public policy arguments weigh in favour of expanding absolute privilege to protect reports made to the police. In the English case *Westcott v Westcott* (2008), Sarah Westcott made a police report stating that her father-in-law had assaulted her and her child. The charge was eventually dismissed, and the father-in-law sued Sarah Wescott for defamation. Sarah Westcott argued that, for policy reasons, her report should be protected by absolute privilege. The courts agreed:

> In order to have confidence that protection will be afforded, the potential complainant must know in advance of making an approach to the police that her complaint will be immune from a direct or a flank attack. There is no logic in conferring immunity at the end of the process but not from the very beginning of the process ... In my judgment immunity must be given from the earliest moment that the criminal justice system becomes involved. It follows that the occasion of the making of both the oral complaint and the subsequent written complaint must be absolutely privileged.[15]

Similar legislative reform is necessary in Canada to protect those who report sexual violence from retaliatory lawsuits and to potentially reduce retaliatory lawsuits from being filed in the first place. The Canadian Centre for Legal Innovation in Sexual Assault Response is currently conducting legal research, led by civil litigator and sexual violence expert Joanna Birenbaum, to examine the possibility of absolute privilege covering formal reports to the police.

Since I began this research, I am regularly asked by people if they risk being sued for silence breaking. The problem is, as I have hopefully demonstrated throughout this book, if someone wants to threaten or initiate legal proceedings, nothing is stopping them. The silence breaker can be careful and follow societal expectations of the ideal victim to the letter, and it won't necessarily matter. For example, she could make a report to the police or a confidential report to human resources or her campus administration and she would still not be protected from someone initiating legal action.

Alternatively, silence breakers aware of the shortcomings of the criminal legal system in sexual assault cases may choose instead to seek an alternative form of justice, such as an accountability process facilitated by a group of friends. The accused can still deny said allegations and sue the silence breaker and, for that matter, everyone who participates in the accountability process. A lawsuit, regardless of the outcome, challenges the silence breaker's narrative and recasts her as mentally ill, a liar, a false accuser, a jilted ex-lover, all while inflicting emotional, financial, and reputational harm upon her. In many ways, a defamation lawsuit is the ideal tool for the abusive man.

Canadians need to know that formal reports are not protected from civil legal actions. I want silence breakers to be aware that while some provinces have anti-SLAPP legislation, the process to have the matter heard in front of a judge is expensive and time-consuming. Most importantly, the courts continue to rely on patriarchal ideologies that value the sanctity of men's reputations over the safety of women and gender-diverse people and their important contributions to public discourse.

I also want to stress that I don't think the threat of a lawsuit should keep people silent – especially not bystanders who are in a position of privilege. When someone asks me if they should break their silence and risk the possibility of a lawsuit, I am reminded of the lawyer who said to me in an interview, "You can be sued for defamation – but – people trot that out as if that is the answer to the question or an insurmountable obstacle." The potential silencing of sexual violence out of a fear of being sued is far worse than being sued. At the same time, I worry about those who report or make a disclosure of sexual violence truly believing that the institution will protect them.

Knowing what I know now, I often hesitate when someone asks, "But will he sue me?," regardless of whether they are asking about reporting to the police, writing a memoir about their experiences of sexual violence, creating an artwork about their experience of reporting to the university, or publicly declaring themselves a survivor. The answer is yes. He can sue because Canadian defamation law allows it and makes it easy to initiate civil legal action regardless of whether the case has merit. But I do think that people, especially those with privilege, should not allow a lawsuit to deter them from supporting those who have experienced sexual violence. Ultimately, we need to ensure that sexual violence discourse does not become reprivatized solely because we fear a possible lawsuit, which is the underlying intention of such lawsuits. Just as abusive men and patriarchal institutions have sought to silence sexual violence discourse, feminist activists and scholars must continue to organize, at a systemic level, to protect silence breakers from retaliatory lawsuits.

Law and Society Series
W. Wesley Pue, Founding Editor

We pay tribute to the late Wes Pue, under whose broad vision, extraordinary leadership, and unwavering commitment to sociolegal studies our Law and Society Series was established and rose to prominence.

The Law and Society Series explores law as a socially embedded phenomenon. It is premised on the understanding that the conventional division of law from society creates false dichotomies in thinking, scholarship, educational practice, and social life. Books in the series treat law and society as mutually constitutive and seek to bridge scholarship emerging from interdisciplinary engagement of law with disciplines such as politics, social theory, history, political economy, and gender studies.

Recent books in the series:

Emilie Biland, translated by Annelies Fryberger and Miranda Richmond Mouillot, *Family Law in Action: Divorce and Inequality in Quebec and France* (2023)
Kate Puddister and Emmett Macfarlane, eds., *Constitutional Crossroads: Reflections on Charter Rights, Reconciliation, and Change* (2022)
Derek Silva and Liam Kennedy, eds., *Power Played: A Critical Criminology of Sport* (2022)
Erez Aloni and Régine Tremblay, eds., *House Rules: Changing Families, Evolving Norms, and the Role of the Law* (2022)
Florence Ashley, *Banning Transgender Conversion Practices: A Legal and Policy Analysis* (2022)
Dia Dabby, *Religious Diversity in Canadian Public Schools: Rethinking the Role of Law* (2022)
Kim Stanton, *Reconciling Truths: Reimagining Public Inquiries in Canada* (2021)
Daniel Rück, *The Laws and the Land: The Settler Colonial Invasion of Kahnawà:ke in Nineteenth-Century Canada* (2021)

For a complete list of the titles in the series, see the UBC Press website, www.ubcpress.ca.

Notes

Disclaimer

1 Joanna Bourke, *Rape: A History from 1860 to the Present Day* (London: Virago, 2010), 6.
2 Bourke, *Rape*.

Preface

1 Kristy Hoffman, "York University's Sexual Assault Policy Sparks Human Rights Complaint," *Globe and Mail*, June 30, 2015, https://www.theglobeandmail.com/news/national/education/york-universitys-sexual-assault-policy-sparks-human-rights-complaint/article25194134/; and Mandi Gray, "Six Lessons I Learned from My Rape Case," *NOW Toronto*, July 26, 2016, https://nowtoronto.com/news/mandi-gray-six-lessons-i-learned-from-my-rape-case/.
2 Tracy Sherlock, "Author Steven Galloway No Longer a UBC Professor following 'Breach of Trust,'" *PostMedia*, June 22, 2016, https://vancouversun.com/news/local-news/steven-galloway-no-longer-a-professor-at-ubc.
3 Deborah Dundas, "Fired Author Steven Galloway Awarded $167,000 in Damages from UBC," *Toronto Star*, June 8, 2018, https://www.thestar.com/entertainment/books/2018/06/08/fired-author-steven-galloway-awarded-167000-in-damages-from-ubc.html.
4 Marsha Lederman, "Court Ruling Supports Steven Galloway's Request for Documents in Defamation Case," *Globe and Mail*, April 10, 2020, https://www.theglobeandmail.com/canada/british-columbia/article-court-ruling-supports-steven-galloways-request-for-documents-in/.
5 Laura Kane, "Margaret Atwood Compares UBC Probe of Steven Galloway to Salem Witch Trials," *Canadian Press*, November 17, 2016, https://www.thestar.com/news/canada/2016/11/17/atwood-compares-ubcs-handling-of-steven-galloway-probe-to-salem-witch-trials.html.

6 Mandi Gray, "How Margaret Atwood Got in Trouble with the 'Good Feminists,'" *NOW Toronto*, February 1, 2018, https://nowtoronto.com/news/is-margaret-atwood-a-bad-feminist..

Introduction

1 See Mandi Gray, "Six Lessons I Learned from My Rape Case," *NOW Toronto*, July 26, 2016, https://nowtoronto.com/news/mandi-gray-six-lessons-i-learned-from-my-rape-case; Kristy Hoffman, "York University's Sexual Assault Policy Sparks Human Rights Complaint," *Globe and Mail*, June 30, 2015, https://www.theglobeandmail.com/news/national/education/york-universitys-sexual-assault-policy-sparks-human-rights-complaint/article25194134/.

2 In 2006, Tarana Burke coined the phrase "Me Too" on the now-defunct social media platform Myspace in reference to her work with young women of colour who had experienced sexual violence. See Aisha Harris, "She Founded Me Too: Now She Wants to Move Past the Trauma," *New York Times*, October 15, 2018, https://www.nytimes.com/2018/10/15/arts/tarana-burke-metoo-anniversary.html.

3 Julia Jacobs, "#MeToo Cases' New Legal Battleground: Defamation Lawsuits," *New York Times*, January 12, 2020, https://www.nytimes.com/2020/01/12/arts/defamation-me-too.html.

4 Jacobs, "#MeToo Cases."

5 Irene Khan, *Gender Justice and Freedom of Expression – Report of the Special Rapporteur on the Promotion and Protection of the Right to Freedom of Opinion and Expression*, United Nations, July 30, 2021, para 22, https://www.ohchr.org/en/documents/thematic-reports/a76258-gender-justice-and-freedom-expression-report-special-rapporteur.

6 Rodrigo Perez Ortega, "Peruvian Scientist Accused of Sexual Harassment Wins Defamation Judgment," *Science*, May 27, 2022, https://www.science.org/content/article/accuser-loses-defamation-suit-peruvian-sexual-harassment-case; Sui-Lee Wee and Li Yuan, "They Said #MeToo: Now They Are Being Sued," *New York Times*, November 3, 2021, https://www.nytimes.com/2019/12/26/business/china-sexual-harassment-metoo.html; Claire Lee, "How #MeToo Movement Is Pushing for Revision of South Korea's Defamation Law," *Korea Herald*, March 1, 2018, http://m.koreaherald.com/view.php?ud=20180301000196; Ayshee Bhaduri, "Bollywood Actor Shilpa Shetty, Raj Kundra File ₹50 Crore Defamation Suit against Sherlyn Chopra," *Hindu Times*, October 19, 2021, https://www.hindustantimes.com/cities/mumbai-news/bollywood-actor-shilpa-shetty-raj-kundra-file-rs-50-crore-defamation-suit-against-sherlyn-chopra-101634651433177.html; Jessica Lake, "McLachlan's Defamation Retreat Won't Stop Other Men Suing to Silence Women," *Sydney Morning Herald*, May 22, 2022, https://www.smh.com.au/national/mclachlan-s-defamation-retreat-won-t-stop-other-men-suing-to-silence-women-20220520-p5an7r.html; Human Rights Law Centre,

"High Court of England and Wales Dismisses a Defamation Claim Brought by a Governor following Sexual Harassment Claims," *Human Rights Law Centre,* November 10, 2017, https://www.hrlc.org.au/human-rights-case-summaries/2018/11/20/high-court-of-england-and-wales-dismisses-a-defamation-claim-brought-by-a-governor-following-sexual-harassment-claims; and Gaspard Sebag and Hugo Miller, "Woman Who Invented French MeToo Hashtag Wins Defamation Suit," *Bloomberg News,* May 11, 2022, https://www.bloomberg.com/news/articles/2022-05-11/woman-who-invented-france-s-metoo-hashtag-wins-defamation-suit.

7 Mike Miller, "Brett Ratner Sues Woman for Defamation over Rape Allegation," *People,* November 1, 2017, https://people.com/movies/brett-ratner-sues-woman-for-defamation-over-rape-allegation/; Angelique Chrisafis, "Feminist Campaigner Accuses Oxford Professor of Rape," *Guardian,* October 22, 2017, https://www.theguardian.com/world/2017/oct/22/feminist-campaigner-accuses-oxford-professor-tariq-ramadan; Nicole Bitette, "Shark Tank Star Robert Herjavec's Ex-girlfriend Claims in Lawsuit That He Repeatedly Raped Her," *Toronto Star,* November 9, 2017, https://www.thestar.com/entertainment/television/2017/11/09/shark-tank-star-robert-herjavecs-ex-girlfriend-claims-in-lawsuit-that-he-repeatedly-raped-her.html; Canadian Press, "Reporter Paul Bliss Was Fired for Repeated Allegations of Sexual Misconduct, CTV Says," *CBC News,* April 2, 2019, https://www.cbc.ca/news/canada/toronto/reporter-paul-bliss-was-fired-for-repeated-allegations-of-sexual-misconduct-ctv-says-1.5082324; Joseph Brean, "Shamed by #MeToo Allegations, Canadian Poet Sues His Accusers, and Media Who Reported Story," *National Post,* July 12, 2018, https://nationalpost.com/news/canada/shamed-by-metoo-allegations-canadian-poet-sues-his-accusers-and-media-who-reported-story; Jacobs, "#MeToo Cases"; Elise Brisco, "Phoebe Bridgers Responds to Defamation Lawsuit from Former Producer Chris Nelson," *USA Today,* February 15, 2022, https://www.usatoday.com/story/entertainment/music/2022/02/15/phoebe-bridgers-responds-chris-nelson-lawsuit-motion-strike/6799238001/; Doha Madani and Diana Dasrath, "Marilyn Manson Files Defamation Lawsuit against Evan Rachel Wood over Rape and Abuse Allegations," *NBC News,* March 2, 2022, https://www.nbcnews.com/pop-culture/pop-culture-news/marilyn-manson-files-defamation-lawsuit-evan-rachel-wood-rape-abuse-al-rcna18436; and Thomas Reuters, "Justin Bieber Files $20M Defamation Lawsuit over Sexual Misconduct Claims," *CBC News,* June 26, 2020, https://www.cbc.ca/news/entertainment/justin-bieber-defamation-lawsuit-sexual-misconduct-1.5629552.

8 Corinne Heller, "Dr. Luke and Kesha's Legal Battle Gets Even Nastier: What They're Claiming Now," *E! News,* November 30, 2018, https://www.eonline.com/news/992010/dr-luke-and-kesha-s-legal-battle-gets-even-nastier-what-they-re-claiming-now; and Phoebe Lett, "Taylor Swift's Priceless Dollar," *New York Times,* August 16, 2017, https://www.nytimes.com/2017/08/16/opinion/taylor-swift-groping-assault.html.

9 Jacob Sarkisian, Zac Ntim, and Ayomikun Adekaiyero, "A Complete Timeline of Johnny Depp and Amber Heard's Tumultuous Relationship," *Insider,* July 15, 2022, https://www.insider.com/johnny-depp-amber-heard-relationship-timeline-2020-7.

10 Amber Heard, "I Spoke Up against Sexual Violence – and Faced Our Culture's Wrath: That Has to Change," *Washington Post,* December 18, 2018, https://www.washingtonpost.com/opinions/ive-seen-how-institutions-protect-men-accused-of-abuse-heres-what-we-can-do/2018/12/18/71fd876a-02ed-11e9-b5df-5d3874f1ac36_story.html.

11 Farrah Khan and Mandi Gray, "Amber Heard Roasting Reveals Harmful Views about Intimate Partner Violence," *Toronto Star,* June 1, 2022, https://www.thestar.com/opinion/contributors/2022/05/31/amber-heard-roasting-reveals-harmful-views-about-intimate-partner-violence.html.

12 Joshua Espinoza, "Content Creators Say Johnny Depp Fans Are Creating 'Hostile Online Environment,'" *Complex,* June 3, 2022, https://www.complex.com/pop-culture/content-creators-say-johnny-depps-fans-are-toxic-domestic-abuse-survivors.

13 Merrit Kennedy, "Amber Heard Said She Has Decided to Settle Johnny Depp's Case against Her," *NPR,* December 19, 2022, https://www.npr.org/2022/12/19/1144132687/amber-heard-johnny-depp-settlement.

14 Jacobs, "#MeToo Cases."

15 Penelope Canan and George Pring, "Strategic Lawsuits against Public Participation," *Social Problems* 35, 5 (1988): 506–19.

16 David Lisak, Lori Gardinier, Sarah C. Nicksa, and Ashley M. Cote, "False Allegations of Sexual Assault: An Analysis of Ten Years of Reported Cases," *Violence against Women* 16, 12 (2010): 1318–34, https://doi.org/10.1177/1077801210387747.

17 Philip H. Osborne, *The Law of Torts,* 5th ed., Essentials of Canadian Law (Toronto: Irwin Law, 2015), 427.

18 Jennifer Freyd, "Violations of Power, Adaptive Blindness and Betrayal Trauma Theory," *Feminist Psychology* 7, 1 (1997): 22–32.

19 Freyd, "Violations of Power," 22–32.

20 Sarah Banet-Weiser, "'Ruined' Lives: Mediated White Male Victimhood," *European Journal of Cultural Studies* 24, 1 (2021): 60–80, https://doi.org/10.1177/1367549420985840.

21 Anna North, "#HimToo, the Online Movement Spreading Myths about False Rape Allegations, Explained," *Vox,* October 10, 2018, https://www.vox.com/policy-and-politics/2018/10/10/17957126/himtoo-movement-pieter-hanson-tweet-me-too.

22 North, "#HimToo."

23 North, "#HimToo."

24 See Christie Blatchford, "Unlike Canada, U.K. Has Learned Sex Assault 'Victims' Aren't Always Victims," *National Post,* April 2, 2018, https://nationalpost.com/opinion/christie-blatchford-unlike-canada-u-k-has-learned-sex-assault-victims-arent

-always-victims; Barbara Kay, "A Sadly Necessary Handbook for Men Falsely Accused of Sexual Assault," *National Post,* December 19, 2017, https://nationalpost.com/opinion/barbara-kay-a-sadly-necessary-handbook-for-men-falsely-accused-of-sexual-assault; Jonathan Kay, "'Grope-Gate' and #MeToo's Crisis of Legitimacy," *Quilette,* July 10, 2018, https://quillette.com/2018/07/10/grope-gate-and-metoos-crisis-of-legitimacy/; and Adam Zivo, "Ruling That Steven Galloway Can Sue over False Allegations a Win for Due Process," *National Post,* December 7, 2021, https://nationalpost.com/opinion/adam-zivo-ruling-that-steven-galloway-can-sue-over-false-rape-allegations-a-win-for-due-process.

25 Constance Backhouse, interview with author, March 19, 2019.
26 David Lisak, Lori Gardinier, Sarah C. Nicksa, and Ashley M. Cote, "False Allegations of Sexual Assault: An Analysis of Ten Years of Reported Cases," *Violence against Women* 16, 12 (2010): 1318–34 (emphasis in original), https://doi.org/10.1177/1077801210387747; and International Association of Chiefs of Police, "Investigating Sexual Assaults: Model Policy," IACP National Law Enforcement Policy Centre, July 2005, 12–13, http://www.evawintl.org/library/DocumentLibraryHandler.ashx?id=328, accessed August 10, 2020.
27 Leigh Gilmore, *Tainted Witness: Why We Doubt What Women Say about Their Lives* (New York: Columbia University Press, 2017).
28 Robyn Doolittle, "Unfounded: Why Police Dismiss 1 in 5 Sexual Assault Claims as Baseless," *Globe and Mail,* February 3, 2017, https://www.theglobeandmail.com/news/investigations/unfounded-sexual-assault-canada-main/article33891309/.
29 Statistics Canada, "Uniform Crime Reporting Incident Based Survey," March 2006, 27, http://www23.statcan.gc.ca/imdb-bmdi/instrument/3302_Q7_V2-eng.pdf.
30 Doolittle, "Unfounded."
31 Doolittle, "Unfounded."
32 A. Blair Crew, "Striking Back: The Viability of a Civil Action against the Police for the 'Wrongful Unfounding' of Reported Rapes," in *Sexual Assault in Canada: Law, Legal Practice and Women's Activism* (Ottawa: University of Ottawa Press, 2012), 211–42; and Elizabeth Sheehy, Sabrina Heyde, and Sunny Marriner, "Please Stop Shaming Women Who Report Sex Assault," *Ottawa Citizen,* August 16, 2017, https://ottawacitizen.com/opinion/columnists/please-stop-shaming-women-who-report-sex-assault.
33 Ronet Bachman, "The Factors Related to Rape Reporting Behavior and Arrest: New Evidence from the National Crime Victimization Survey," *Criminal Justice and Behavior* 25, 1 (1998): 8–29, https://doi.org/10.1177/0093854898025001002.
34 Adam Cotter and Laura Savage, "Gender-Based Violence and Unwanted Sexual Behaviour in Canada, 2018: Initial Findings from the Survey of Safety in Public and Private Spaces," Statistics Canada, December 5, 2019, https://www150.statcan.gc.ca/n1/pub/85-002-x/2019001/article/00017-eng.htm.

35 Cotter and Savage, "Gender-Based Violence."
36 Bachman, "The Factors Related to Rape Reporting Behavior and Arrest."
37 Catherine C. Classen, Oxana Gronskaya Palesh, and Rashi Aggarwal, "Sexual Revictimization: A Review of the Empirical Literature," *Trauma, Violence, and Abuse* 6, 2 (2005): 103–29, https://doi.org/10.1177/1524838005275087; and Jodie Murphy-Oikonen, Lori Chambers, Karen McQueen, Alexa Hiebert, and Ainsley Miller, "Sexual Assault: Indigenous Women's Experiences of Not Being Believed by the Police," *Violence against Women* 28, 5 (2021): 1035–76, https://doi.org/10.1177/10778012211013903.
38 Murphy-Oikonen et al., "Sexual Assault."
39 For a more nuanced discussion on how social location influences the decision to report or disclose sexual violence, see Sarah Jane Brubaker, Brittany Keegan, Xavier L. Guadalupe-Diaz, and Bre'Auna Beasley, "Measuring and Reporting Campus Sexual Assault: Privilege and Exclusion in What We Know and What We Do," *Sociology Compass* 11, 12 (2017): https://doi.org/10.1111/soc4.12543; Murphy-Oikonen et al., "Sexual Assault"; and Brittany C. Slatton and April L. Richard, "Black Women's Experiences of Sexual Assault and Disclosure: Insights from the Margins," *Sociology Compass* 14, 6 (2020): https://doi/10.1111/soc4.12792.
40 Jason Proctor, "Appeal of Steven Galloway Lawsuit Pits Author's Fight for Reputation against Accuser's Right to Speak Out," *CBC News,* February 13, 2022, https://www.cbc.ca/news/canada/british-columbia/galloway-sexual-assault-defamation-appeal-1.6342820.
41 Anastasia Powell, "Seeking Informal Justice Online: Vigilanteism, Activism and Resisting a Rape Culture in Cyber Space," in *Rape Justice: Beyond the Criminal Law,* ed. Anastasia Powell, Nicola Henry, and Asher Flynn (London: Palgrave Macmillan, 2015), 218–37.
42 adrienne maree brown, *We Will Not Cancel Us: Breaking the Cycle of Harm,* Emergent Strategy Series 4 (Chico, CA: AK Press, 2020); Mia Mingus, "Transformative Justice: A Brief Description," *Leaving Evidence* (blog), January 9, 2019, https://leavingevidence.wordpress.com/2019/01/09/transformative-justice-a-brief-description/; Kai Cheng Thom, *I Hope We Choose Love: A Trans Girl's Notes from the End of the World* (Vancouver: Arsenal Pulp Press, 2019); Angela Cameron, "Stopping the Violence: Canadian Feminist Debates on Restorative Justice and Intimate Violence," *Theoretical Criminology* 10, 1 (2006): 49–66; Clare McGlynn, Nicole Westmarland, and Nikki Godden, "'I Just Wanted Him to Hear Me': Sexual Violence and the Possibilities of Restorative Justice," *Journal of Law and Society* 39, 2 (2012): 213–40, https://doi.org/10.1111/j.1467-6478.2012.00579.x; and Powell, "Seeking Informal Justice Online."
43 Byron M. Sheldrick, *Blocking Public Participation: The Use of Strategic Litigation to Silence Political Expression* (Waterloo, ON: Wilfrid Laurier University Press, 2014).

44 Cotter and Savage, "Gender-Based Violence."
45 Debra Delaet and Elizabeth Mills, "Discursive Silence as a Global Response to Sexual Violence: From Title IX to Truth Commissions," *Global Society* 32, 4 (2018): 497.
46 Cheryl Glenn, *Unspoken: A Rhetoric of Silence* (Carbondale: Southern Illinois University Press, 2004), 2.
47 Linda Martín Alcoff, *Rape and Resistance: Understanding the Complexities of Sexual Violation* (Cambridge: Polity, 2018).
48 bell hooks, *Talking Back: Thinking Feminist, Thinking Black* (Boston: South End Press, 1989), 9.
49 Stephanie Zacharek, Eliana Dockterman, and Haley Sweetland Edwards, "The Silence Breakers," *TIME*, December 18, 2017, http://time.com/time-person-of-the-year-2017-silence-breakers/.
50 Zacharek, Dockterman, and Sweetland Edwards, "The Silence Breakers."
51 These categories are somewhat arbitrary. For example, I interviewed Julie Macfarlane, who is a law professor but who was also sued by a former colleague accused of sexual harassment. For this reason, I have listed her as a silence breaker as opposed to a law professor. In another instance, I interviewed a law professor because of her extensive knowledge of the feminist movement in Canada and because she referenced a defamation lawsuit against a woman who reported sexual harassment in the 1980s. During the interview, she disclosed that she had been sued for defamation early in her career. She provided valuable insights about the challenges of being a defendant named on a lawsuit, but the lawsuit itself was not directly tied to sexual violence. Because of this, I categorized her as a law professor, but, in many ways, she was a silence breaker.
52 Laura L. Starzynski, Sarah E. Ullman, Henrietta H. Filipas, and Stephanie Townsend, "Correlates of Women's Sexual Assault Disclosure to Informal and Formal Support Sources," *Violence and Victims* 20, 4 (2005): 417–32, https://doi.org/10.1891/0886-6708.20.4.417.
53 Etienne G. Krug, Linda L. Dahlberg, James A. Mercy, Anthony B. Zwi, and Rafael Lozano, *World Report on Violence and Health* (Geneva: World Health Organization, 2002), 149, https://apps.who.int/iris/bitstream/handle/10665/42495/9241545615_eng.pdf.
54 Jessica A. Turchik, Claire L. Hebenstreit, and Stephanie S. Judson, "An Examination of the Gender Inclusiveness of Current Theories of Sexual Violence in Adulthood: Recognizing Male Victims, Female Perpetrators, and Same-Sex Violence," *Trauma, Violence, and Abuse* 17, 2 (2016): 133–48, https://doi.org/10.1177/1524838014566721.
55 Shana Conroy and Adam Cotter, "Self-Reported Sexual Assault in Canada," Statistics Canada, July 11, 2017, https://www150.statcan.gc.ca/n1/pub/85-002-x/2017001/article/14842-eng.htm.
56 KelleyAnne Malinen, "'This Was a Sexual Assault': A Social Worlds Analysis of Paradigm Change in the Interpersonal Violence World," *Symbolic Interaction* 37, 3

(2014): 353–68, https://doi.org/10.1002/symb.103; and Turchik, Hebenstreit, and Judson, "An Examination of the Gender Inclusiveness of Current Theories of Sexual Violence in Adulthood."

57 Elizabeth Comack and Gillian Balfour, *The Power to Criminalize: Violence, Inequality and Law* (Halifax: Fernwood, 2004); Elaine Craig, *Putting Trials on Trial: Sexual Assault and the Failure of the Legal Profession* (Montreal/Kingston: McGill-Queen's University Press, 2018); Jane Doe, *The Story of Jane Doe: A Book about Rape* (Toronto: Random House Canada, 2003); Tracy Lindberg, Priscilla Campeau, and Maria Campbell, "Indigenous Women and Sexual Assault in Canada," in *Sexual Assault in Canada: Law, Legal Practice and Women's Activism*, ed. Elizabeth Sheehy (Ottawa: University of Ottawa Press, 2012), 87–110; and Fran Odette, "Sexual Assault and Disabled Women Ten Years after *Jane Doe*," in Sheehy, *Sexual Assault in Canada*, 173–90.

Chapter 1: A Civil Law Primer

1 Osler, Hoskin & Harcourt LLP, "Introductory Guide to Civil Litigation in Ontario," 2018. I rely on the Ontario Rules of Civil Procedure simply because this study was based in Ontario, and it is the most populous province in the country. See Revised Regulations of Ontario (RRO) 1990, Reg 194, Rules of Civil Procedure, https://www.ontario.ca/laws/regulation/900194.

2 Noel Semple, "The Cost of Seeking Civil Justice in Canada," *Canadian Bar Review* 93, 3 (2016): 639–73.

3 *Limitations Act*, SO 2002, c 24, Schedule B, https://www.ontario.ca/laws/statute/02l24/v25. The exception is if the libel was published by a newsroom or a broadcaster, in which case the action must be initiated within three months "after the libel has come to the knowledge of the person defamed" (RSO 1990, s 6).

4 RRO 1990, Reg 194, s 16.

5 A peace bond is a protection order made by a court under s 810 of the Criminal Code, https://laws-lois.justice.gc.ca/eng/acts/C-46/section-810.html.

6 Ali was served before a major religious holiday, while Catherine and Morgan were both served on a Friday afternoon. This tactic is not unusual. Other research participants reported receiving legal notices late on a Friday evening. Another received theirs right before the Christmas holidays began. While this may be a coincidence, lawyers shared with me that plaintiffs and their lawyers sometimes do this to make it difficult for the defendant to connect with a lawyer or simply to ruin any holidays or plans they may have.

7 Ontario Ministry of the Attorney General, "Civil Cases: Suing and Being Sued in the Superior Court of Justice," n.d., https://www.attorneygeneral.jus.gov.on.ca/english/courts/civil/suing_and_being_sued_7.php.

8 RRO 1990, Reg 194, s 18.01(a)(b).
9 RRO 1990, Reg 194, r 19.01(1).
10 RRO 1990, Reg 194, r 19.02.
11 Statistics Canada, Table 35-10-0112-01, "Civil Court Cases, by Level of Court and Type of Case, Canada and Selected Provinces and Territories," https://doi.org/10.25318/3510011201-eng.
12 Legal information is more general and provides an explanation of the law, the legal system, or legal terminology. "Legal advice" refers to advice from a lawyer or paralegal about a specific legal problem.
13 Erin York Cornwell, Emily S. Taylor Poppe, and Megan Doherty Bea, "Networking in the Shadow of the Law: Informal Access to Legal Expertise through Personal Network Ties," *Law and Society Review* 51, 3 (2017): 635–68, https://doi.org/10.1111/lasr.12278.
14 All Canadian jurisdictions follow the "loser pays" rule, meaning that the person who loses is required to pay the fees and costs of the winning party. That being said, the amount is determined by the court, and the full amount will never be awarded. Furthermore, even if costs are awarded, there may be difficulties retrieving the money.
15 Janet Elizabeth Walker and Lorne Mitchell Sossin, *Civil Litigation,* Essentials of Canadian Law (Toronto: Irwin Law, 2010), 169.
16 Walker and Sossin, *Civil Litigation,* 169.
17 Walker and Sossin, *Civil Litigation,* 170.
18 Walker and Sossin, *Civil Litigation,* 170.
19 RRO 1990, Reg 194, r 30.02.
20 RRO 1990, Reg 194, r 30.01[a].
21 Walker and Sossin, *Civil Litigation,* 171.
22 Walker and Sossin, *Civil Litigation,* 171.
23 Walker and Sossin, *Civil Litigation,* 171.
24 BC Justice Review Task Force, "Effective and Affordable Civil Justice: Report of the Civil Justice Reform Working Group to the Justice Review Task Force," November 2006, 25, https://www2.gov.bc.ca/assets/gov/law-crime-and-justice/about-bc-justice-system/justice-reform-initiatives/cjrwg_report_11_06.pdf. "Privilege" refers to the protection of certain communications, specifically those protected and shared for a social or moral reason. Chapter 2, this volume, provides a more in-depth explanation of the legal concept and significance of privilege in defamation lawsuits.
25 Walker and Sossin, *Civil Litigation,* 177.
26 Walker and Sossin, *Civil Litigation,* 178.
27 Walker and Sossin, *Civil Litigation,* 178.
28 Karen Busby, "Discriminatory Uses of Personal Records in Sexual Violence Cases," *Canadian Journal of Women and the Law* 9, 2 (1997): 148–76; Elizabeth Comack and

Gillian Balfour, *The Power to Criminalize: Violence, Inequality and Law* (Halifax: Fernwood, 2004); Elaine Craig, *Putting Trials on Trial: Sexual Assault and the Failure of the Legal Profession* (Montreal/Kingston: McGill-Queen's University Press, 2018); Lise Gotell, "When Privacy Is Not Enough: Sexual Assault Complainants, Sexual History Evidence and the Disclosure of Personal Records," *Alberta Law Review* 43, 3 (2006): 743–78; and David Ward, "In Her Words: Recognizing and Preventing Abusive Litigation against Domestic Violence Survivors," *Seattle Journal for Social Justice* 14, 2 (2016): 429–64.

29 Gotell, "When Privacy Is Not Enough," 772.
30 Gotell, "When Privacy Is Not Enough," 774.
31 Constance Backhouse, interview with author, March 19, 2019.
32 Weyman Lundquist and Frank F. Flegal, "Discovery Abuse: Some New Views about an Old Problem," *Review of Litigation* 2, 1 (1981): 6.
33 I could access this transcript because Marilou McPhedran donated her lawsuit materials, including the discovery transcript, to the Clara Thomas Archives at York University.
34 Lisa Priest, "Task Force to Probe Abuse by Health-Care Workers: Province Wants Team to Investigate Whether Survivors Feel Penalties Meted Out to Abusers Are 'Fair and Just,' Witmer Says," *Globe and Mail,* February 16, 2000.
35 Marilou McPhedran, "First, Do No Harm: A Decade Ago, a Task Force Recommended Zero Tolerance of Sexual Abuse by Doctors. The Policy's Effect? Close to Zero," *Globe and Mail,* June 21, 2001.
36 Zena Olijnyk, "Legal Services in a Most Unusual Year: 2021 Legal Fees Survey," *Canadian Lawyer,* May 25, 2021, https://www.canadianlawyermag.com/surveys-reports/legal-fees/legal-services-in-a-most-unusual-year-2021-legal-fees-survey/356483.
37 Marge Bruineman, "Steady Optimism: 2019 Legal Fees Survey," *Canadian Lawyer,* April 8, 2019, https://www.canadianlawyermag.com/surveys-reports/legal-fees/steady-optimism-2019-legal-fees-survey/276027.
38 When I connected with Laura to verify the accuracy of the quotes, Laura laughed as I read this quote to her because, in retrospect, she felt she'd been naive about the real costs of retaining legal counsel. After she spoke to me, she received quotes from lawyers estimating it would cost $100,000 to $200,000 to litigate.
39 Philip H. Osborne, *The Law of Torts,* 5th ed., Essentials of Canadian Law (Toronto: Irwin Law, 2015).
40 Osler, Hoskin & Harcourt LLP, "Introductory Guide to Civil Litigation in Ontario."
41 Department of Justice, "Civil and Criminal Cases," *Canada's System of Justice* (blog), October 16, 2017, https://www.justice.gc.ca/eng/csj-sjc/just/08.html.
42 Osler, Hoskin & Harcourt LLP, "Introductory Guide to Civil Litigation in Ontario."
43 Osler, Hoskin & Harcourt LLP, "Introductory Guide to Civil Litigation in Ontario," 11.

44 Lisa Taylor, "How the Criminal Code 'Protects' Sexual Assault Complainants from Themselves and Constrains Their Participation in the News Media," in *The Unfulfilled Promise of Press Freedom in Canada*, ed. Lisa Taylor and Cara-Marie O'Hagan (Toronto: University of Toronto Press, 2017), 132–45. The complainant can apply to the courts to have the publication ban rescinded, but there is no guarantee that the court will comply.
45 *Canadian Newspapers Co. v Canada (Attorney General)* [1988] 2 SCR 122, 1988 SCC 52 [*Canadian Newspapers*], http://canlii.ca/t/1ftdc.
46 *Canadian Newspapers*, para 15.
47 Jane Doe, "What's in a Name? Who Benefits from the Publication Ban in Sexual Assault Trials," in *Lessons from the Identity Trail: Anonymity, Privacy and Identity in a Networked Society*, ed. Ian Kerr, Valerie Steeves, and Carole Lucock (New York: Oxford University Press, 2009), 265–81; Craig, *Putting Trials on Trial*; and Taylor, "How the Criminal Code 'Protects' Sexual Assault Complainants."
48 *Galloway v A.B.*, 2019 BCSC 395 [*Galloway*], http://canlii.ca/t/hznmr; and *Stuart v Doe*, 2019 YKSC 53 [*Stuart*], http://canlii.ca/t/j34c1.
49 Jackie Hong, "Fired Yukon College Instructor Sues Student over Sex Assault Allegations," *Yukon News*, October 26, 2018, https://www.yukon-news.com/news/fired-yukon-college-instructor-sues-student-over-sex-assault-allegations/.
50 Requesting a motion for a publication ban adds to the financial burden. The national average for a motion ranges from $5,000 to $10,000.
51 *Stuart*, para 33.
52 *Galloway*, para 11.
53 *Galloway*, para 11.
54 This is not to suggest that Galloway and his supporters have not attempted to disrupt A.B. as a "good victim" in legal documents, in the media, and on social media. Galloway strategically framed A.B. as a "jilted lover" following a failed "affair." Galloway's notice of civil claim and public statements frequently reference the fact that A.B. is older to demonstrate there was no power imbalance between them.

Chapter 2: The Gender of Reputation

1 Cited in David Rolph, *Reputation, Celebrity and Defamation Law* (Aldershot, UK: Ashgate, 2008), 6.
2 *Hill v Church of Scientology of Toronto*, 1995 SCC 59, [1995] 2 SCR 1130 [*Hill*], http://canlii.ca/t/1frgn. The Church of Scientology claimed that Hill, a Crown attorney, misled a judge and breached a court order sealing documents that belonged to the Church of Scientology. The case went to the Supreme Court to assess whether the tort of defamation was inconsistent with the Charter 2(b) right of freedom of expression. The court decided that the law is an appropriate balance between competing interests of reputation and freedom of expression.
3 *Hill*, para 107.

4 Gillian Balfour, "The Practice of Law as Structured Action: The Role of Lawyers in the Criminalization of Violent Men and Women" (PhD diss., University of Manitoba, 2002), https://mspace.lib.umanitoba.ca/xmlui/handle/1993/19791; and Elizabeth Comack and Gillian Balfour, *The Power to Criminalize: Violence, Inequality and Law* (Halifax: Fernwood, 2004), chap. 2.
5 Robert C. Post, "The Social Foundations of Defamation Law: Reputation and the Constitution," *California Law Review* 74, 3 (1986): 691–742.
6 Jerome H. Skolnick, "Foreword: The Sociological Tort of Defamation," *California Law Review* 74, 3 (1986): 677–89.
7 Laura A. Heymann, "The Law of Reputation and Interest of the Audience," *Boston College Law Review* 52, 4 (2011): 1341–440.
8 *Hill*, para 113.
9 Robert Danay, "The Medium Is Not the Message: Reconciling Reputation and Free Expression in Cases of Internet Defamation," *McGill Law Journal* 56, 1 (2010): 23, https://doi.org/10.7202/045697ar.
10 *Hill*, para 117.
11 Danay, "The Medium Is Not the Message," 3.
12 Hilary Young, "The Canadian Defamation Action: An Empirical Study," *Canadian Bar Review* 95, 3 (2017): 593.
13 Danay, "The Medium Is Not the Message"; and Philip H. Osborne, *The Law of Torts*, 5th ed., Essentials of Canadian Law (Toronto: Irwin Law, 2015).
14 Danay, "The Medium Is Not the Message."
15 Danay, "The Medium Is Not the Message."
16 Danay, "The Medium Is Not the Message," 19.
17 Young, "The Canadian Defamation Action." Young also states that there are some exceptions to strict liability under the latest defence of responsible communications, which is grounded in a lack of fault.
18 Danay, "The Medium Is Not the Message," 18.
19 Danay, "The Medium Is Not the Message," 19.
20 Danay, "The Medium Is Not the Message," 19.
21 Young, "The Canadian Defamation Action."
22 Skolnick, "Foreword," 677.
23 Francesca Giardini and Rafael Wittek, eds., "Introduction: Gossip and Reputation – A Multidisciplinary Research Program," in *The Oxford Handbook of Gossip and Reputation*, ed. Francesca Giardini and Rafael Wittek (New York: Oxford University Press, 2019), 1.
24 Heymann, "The Law of Reputation and Interest of the Audience."
25 Heymann, "The Law of Reputation and Interest of the Audience."
26 Heymann, "The Law of Reputation and Interest of the Audience."

27 *Hill*, para 107.
28 *Hill*, para 120.
29 Skolnick, "Foreword."
30 Post, "The Social Foundations of Defamation Law," 693.
31 Post, "The Social Foundations of Defamation Law," 693.
32 Post, "The Social Foundations of Defamation Law," 693.
33 Post, "The Social Foundations of Defamation Law," 695.
34 Heymann, "The Law of Reputation and Interest of the Audience."
35 Heymann, "The Law of Reputation and Interest of the Audience."
36 Heymann, "The Law of Reputation and Interest of the Audience."
37 Heymann, "The Law of Reputation and Interest of the Audience."
38 *Rizvee v Newman*, 2017 ONSC 4024, http://canlii.ca/t/h4npx.
39 Post, "The Social Foundations of Defamation Law."
40 Post, "The Social Foundations of Defamation Law," 707.
41 Post, "The Social Foundations of Defamation Law," 712.
42 Post, "The Social Foundations of Defamation Law," 710.
43 Post, "The Social Foundations of Defamation Law," 710.
44 *R v Lucas*, 1998 1 SCR 439 [*Lucas*], https://canlii.ca/t/1fqt3.
45 *Lucas*, para 48.
46 *Vanderkooy v Vanderkooy et al*, 2013 ONSC 4796, para 215, http://canlii.ca/t/g04cb.
47 *Whitfield v Whitfield*, 2016 ONCA 581, http://canlii.ca/t/gsp2p.
48 Diane L. Borden, "Patterns of Harm: An Analysis of Gender and Defamation," *Communication Law and Policy* 2, 1 (1997): 105–41, https://doi.org/10.1080/10811689709368620; Diane L. Borden, "Reputational Assault: A Critical and Historical Analysis of Gender and the Law of Defamation," *Journalism and Mass Communication Quarterly* 75, 1 (1998): 98–111, https://doi.org/10.1177/107769909807500111; Andrew J. King, "Constructing Gender: Sexual Slander in Nineteenth-Century America," *Law and History Review* 13, 1 (1995): 63–110; Lisa R. Pruitt, "'On the Chastity of Women All Property in the World Depends': Injury from Sexual Slander in the Nineteenth Century," *Indiana Law Journal* 78, 3 (2003): 965–1018; and Lisa R. Pruitt, "Her Own Good Name: Two Centuries of Talk about Chastity," *Maryland Law Review* 63, 3 (2004): 401–539.
49 Borden, "Patterns of Harm"; and Post, "The Social Foundations of Defamation Law."
50 Borden, "Patterns of Harm"; Alice Krzanich, "Virtue and Vindication: An Historical Analysis of Sexual Slander and a Woman's Good Name," *Auckland University Law Review* 17 (2011): 33–59; and Pruitt, "On the Chastity of Women."
51 Borden, "Patterns of Harm"; and Borden, "Reputational Assault."
52 Borden, "Patterns of Harm."

53 Borden, "Patterns of Harm."
54 Borden, "Patterns of Harm."
55 Pruitt, "Her Own Good Name," 470–71.
56 Pruitt, "Her Own Good Name."
57 Pruitt states that "new chastity" cases are seldom successful in the United States because they are ruled a matter of opinion protected by the First Amendment. Unfortunately, to date, there is no similar research examining women's defamation claims in the Canadian context.
58 Pruitt, "Her Own Good Name"; and Borden, "Patterns of Harm."
59 Pruitt, "Her Own Good Name."
60 Lisa Taylor and David Pritchard, "The Process Is the Punishment: Criminal Libel and Political Speech in Canada," *Communication Law and Policy* 23, 3 (2018): 243–66, https://doi.org/10.1080/10811680.2018.1467155. Taylor and Pritchard state that criminal libel has a long history in Canada. The Criminal Code definition has remained relatively unchanged since 1912. By contrast, the number of US states with criminal libel laws has been steadily declining since the 1960s, and the offence has been struck down by the United Kingdom and several former British colonies. While criminal libel is not the focus of the present study, it is an area of law that awaits further research.
61 Criminal Code, s 298(1).
62 Taylor and Pritchard, "The Process Is the Punishment."
63 Taylor and Pritchard, "The Process Is the Punishment."
64 Lewis Mark Webb, "Shame Transfigured: Slut-Shaming from Rome to Cyberspace," *First Monday,* April 2, 2015, https://doi.org/10.5210/fm.v20i4.5464.
65 Although beyond the scope of this study, another interesting finding from their research was that several of the criminal defamation charges were laid following public protests, criticism of police, or allegations of police engaging in sexual violence. Police officers also laid charges against citizens for calling female police officers derogatory and gendered names such as "fat cow," "bitch," and "fucking sow." This finding speaks to the gendered nature of defamation, even in the context of criminal defamation law (Taylor and Pritchard, "The Process Is the Punishment," 255–56). While police officers should not be able to criminalize people for such statements, the gendered language targeting female police officers supports the argument that women are often subjected to gendered reputational damage.
66 Pruitt, "Her Own Good Name."
67 Julia Jacobs, "#MeToo Cases' New Legal Battleground: Defamation Lawsuits," *New York Times,* January 12, 2020, https://www.nytimes.com/2020/01/12/arts/defamation-me-too.html.
68 Jacobs, "#MeToo Cases."

69 Jacobs, "#MeToo Cases."
70 Jacobs, "#MeToo Cases."
71 "Consent" refers to the unusual circumstances in which the plaintiff consented to the publication of defamatory statements.
72 Every province and territory in Canada has its own defamation act, and there are differences among the provinces. For example, Alberta, Manitoba, New Brunswick, Nova Scotia, and Prince Edward Island have abandoned the distinction between libel and slander. Provinces that have maintained this distinction, however, have adjusted the traditional meaning of libel to reflect new technologies. For example, the *Ontario Libel and Slander Act* now includes television and radio broadcasts and print media as sites of potential libel; see Osborne, *Law of Torts*.
73 Osborne, *Law of Torts*.
74 Osborne, *Law of Torts*, 437.
75 Osborne, *Law of Torts*, 437.
76 Osborne, *Law of Torts*, 437.
77 Osborne, *Law of Torts*, 437.
78 Osborne, *Law of Torts*, 437.
79 Lillianne Cadieux-Shaw, "Defamation, Absolute Privilege, and Sexual Assault: Caron v A," *The Court.ca*, March 7, 2015, https://www.thecourt.ca/defamation-absolute-privilege-and-sexual-assault-caron-v-a/.
80 Cadieux-Shaw, "Defamation, Absolute Privilege, and Sexual Assault."
81 Cadieux-Shaw, "Defamation, Absolute Privilege, and Sexual Assault."
82 Cadieux-Shaw, "Defamation, Absolute Privilege, and Sexual Assault."
83 Cadieux-Shaw, "Defamation, Absolute Privilege, and Sexual Assault."
84 Cadieux-Shaw, "Defamation, Absolute Privilege, and Sexual Assault."
85 Cadieux-Shaw, "Defamation, Absolute Privilege, and Sexual Assault."
86 Osborne, *Law of Torts*.
87 Osborne, *Law of Torts*.
88 *Hill*.
89 Osborne, *Law of Torts*.
90 Osborne, *Law of Torts*.
91 Osborne, *Law of Torts*.
92 Osborne, *Law of Torts*.
93 Osborne, *Law of Torts*.
94 *Franchuk v Schick*, 2014 ABQB 249 [*Franchuk*], http://canlii.ca/t/g7rt9.
95 *Franchuk*, para 3.
96 *Franchuk*, para 20.
97 *Franchuk*, para 20.
98 *Franchuk*, para 28.

99 *Franchuk,* para 29.
100 *Whitfield v Whitfield,* 2016 ONCA 581 [*Whitfield,* 2016], http://canlii.ca/t/gsp2p.
101 *Whitfield,* 2016, para 76.
102 *Whitfield v Whitfield,* 2014 ONSC 2745 [*Whitfield,* 2014], http://canlii.ca/t/g6s8v.
103 *Whitfield,* 2016.
104 *Whitfield,* 2016, para 78.
105 *Whitfield,* 2016, para 78.
106 *Whitfield,* 2016, paras 79, 81. It's important to note the power differential here. Bryan Whitfield was represented by a prominent Toronto legal counsel while Agnes Whitfield was self-represented.
107 Osborne, *Law of Torts.*
108 Osborne, *Law of Torts,* 439.
109 Katie Duke, "Calling a Racist a Racist: A Case for Reforming the Tort of Defamation," *Windsor Review of Legal and Social Issues* 37, 70 (2016): 88–89.
110 Osborne, *Law of Torts,* 442.
111 Osborne, *Law of Torts,* 440.
112 Duke, "Calling a Racist a Racist."
113 Duke, "Calling a Racist a Racist."
114 Duke, "Calling a Racist a Racist."
115 Duke, "Calling a Racist a Racist."
116 *Mainstream Canada v Staniford,* 2013 BCCA 341 [*Mainstream*], http://canlii.ca/t/fzqsx.
117 Duke, "Calling a Racist a Racist."
118 *Mainstream,* para 43, cited in Duke, "Calling a Racist a Racist," 90.
119 *Grant,* para 31, cited in Duke, "Calling a Racist a Racist," 90.
120 Duke, "Calling a Racist a Racist."
121 Osborne, *Law of Torts.*
122 *Libel and Slander Act,* RSO 1990, c L 12, s 20, https://www.ontario.ca/laws/statute/90l12.
123 I emailed this journalist for an interview because she had been sued after she said a colleague in the news industry had sexually harassed her. Since she was hoping to settle the lawsuit, she declined the interview request. However, she provided me with the names of two women who had also been sued or threatened with a lawsuit and publicly retracted their statements. I've removed the journalist's name because I was in contact with her during my recruitment efforts, and I want to protect her from potential legal retaliation.
124 Post, "The Social Foundations of Defamation Law."
125 Post, "The Social Foundations of Defamation Law."
126 Post, "The Social Foundations of Defamation Law."

Chapter 3: Sick and Silenced

1. Heidi Rimke, "Sickening Institutions: A Feminist Sociological Analysis and Critique of Religion, Medicine, and Psychiatry," in *Containing Madness*, ed. Jennifer M. Kilty and Erin Dej (London: Palgrave Macmillan, 2018), 15, https://doi.org/10.1007/978 3-319-89749-3_2.
2. Rimke, "Sickening Institutions."
3. Rebecca Campbell and Sheela Raja, "Secondary Victimization of Rape Victims: Insights from Mental Health Professionals Who Treat Survivors of Violence," *Violence and Victims* 14, 1 (1999): 261–75; Sarah E. Ullman, "Sexual Assault Victimization and Suicidal Behavior in Women: A Review of the Literature," *Aggression and Violent Behavior* 9, 4 (2004): 331–51; Sarah E. Ullman and Leanne R. Brecklin, "Sexual Assault History and Health-Related Outcomes in a National Sample of Women," *Psychology of Women Quarterly* 27, 1 (2003): 46–57; Sarah E. Ullman and Henrietta H. Filipas, "Predictors of PTSD Symptom Severity and Social Reactions in Sexual Assault Victims," *Journal of Traumatic Stress* 14, 2 (2001): 369–89; and Sarah E. Ullman and Liana C. Peter-Hagene, "Longitudinal Relationships of Social Reactions, PTSD, and Revictimization in Sexual Assault Survivors," *Journal of Interpersonal Violence* 31, 6 (2016): 1074–94.
4. Jennifer Freyd, "Violations of Power, Adaptive Blindness and Betrayal Trauma Theory," *Feminist Psychology* 7, 1 (1997): 22–32; and Carly Parnitzke Smith and Jennifer J. Freyd, "Dangerous Safe Havens: Institutional Betrayal Exacerbates Sexual Trauma," *Journal of Traumatic Stress* 26, 1 (2013): 119–24, https://doi.org/10.1002/jts.21778.
5. Smith and Freyd, "Dangerous Safe Havens."
6. Smith and Freyd, "Dangerous Safe Havens."
7. Smith and Freyd, "Dangerous Safe Havens."
8. Smith and Freyd, "Dangerous Safe Havens."
9. Marina N. Rosenthal, Alec M. Smidt, and Jennifer J. Freyd, "Still Second Class: Sexual Harassment of Graduate Students," *Psychology of Women Quarterly* 40, 3 (2016): 364–77, https://doi.org/10.1177/0361684316644838.
10. "Suicidal ideation" refers to thoughts of suicide; it does not necessarily mean an individual has attempted suicide.
11. Mandi Gray, "Pathologizing Indigenous Suicide: Examining the Inquest into the Deaths of C.J. and C.B.," *Studies in Social Justice* 10, 1 (2016): 80–94.
12. Kathleen A. Kendall-Tackett, "Inflammation, Cardiovascular Disease, and Metabolic Syndrome as Sequelae of Violence against Women: The Role of Depression, Hostility, and Sleep Disturbance," *Trauma, Violence, and Abuse* 8, 2 (2007): 117–26, https://doi.org/10.1177/1524838007301161.
13. Elaine Craig, *Putting Trials on Trial: Sexual Assault and the Failure of the Legal Profession* (Montreal/Kingston: McGill-Queen's University Press, 2018); Melanie

Randall, "Sexual Assault Law, Credibility, and 'Ideal Victims': Consent, Resistance and Victim Blaming," *Canadian Journal of Women and the Law* 22, 2 (2010): 397–433; and Daniel Tanovich, "'Whack' No More: Infusing Equality into the Ethics of Defence Lawyering in Sexual Assault Cases," *Ottawa Law Review* 45, 3 (2015): 495–525.

14 See Kaitlynn Mendes, Jessica Ringrose, and Jessalynn Keller, "#MeToo and the Promise and Pitfalls of Challenging Rape Culture through Digital Feminist Activism," *European Journal of Women's Studies* 25, 2 (2018): 236–46, https://doi.org/10.1177/1350506818765318; Kaitlynn Mendes, Jessica Ringrose, and Jessalynn Keller, *Digital Feminist Activism: Girls and Women Fight Back against Rape Culture*, Oxford Studies in Digital Politics (New York: Oxford University Press, 2019); Anastasia Powell, "Seeking Rape Justice: Formal and Informal Responses to Sexual Violence through Technosocial Counter-publics," *Theoretical Criminology* 19, 4 (2015): 571–88, https://doi.org/10.1177/1362480615576271; and Sophie Sills, Chelsea Pickens, Karishma Beach, Lloyd Jones, Octavia Calder-Dawe, Paulette Benton-Grieg, and Nicola Gavey, "Rape Culture and Social Media: Young Critics and a Feminist Counterpublic," *Feminist Media Studies* 16, 6 (2016): 935–51, https://doi.org/10.1080/14680777.2015.1137962.

15 Powell, "Seeking Rape Justice."

16 Powell, "Seeking Rape Justice"; Mendes, Ringrose, and Keller, "#MeToo and the Promise and Pitfalls," 236–46; and Mendes, Ringrose, and Keller, *Digital Feminist Activism*.

17 Powell, "Seeking Rape Justice."

18 Anastasia Powell and Nicola Henry, *Sexual Violence in a Digital Age*, Palgrave Studies in Cybercrime and Cybersecurity (London: Palgrave Macmillan, 2017).

19 Powell and Henry, *Sexual Violence in a Digital Age*.

20 At the time of writing, I asked Wanda about the status of the lawsuit against her. As the costs continued to grow, she decided to abandon the lawsuit and let it go to default judgment. Since she does not have any assets, she decided this was the best decision for her and her family. Four years have passed since our initial interview and the case has not yet gone to trial nor has a trial date been set.

21 Julie Macfarlane, "How a Good Idea Became a Bad Idea: Universities and the Use of Non-disclosure Agreements in Terminations for Sexual Misconduct," *Cardozo Journal of Conflict Resolution* 21 (2020): 364.

22 Macfarlane, "How a Good Idea Became a Bad Idea," 361.

23 Macfarlane, "How a Good Idea Became a Bad Idea," 362.

24 Byron M. Sheldrick, *Blocking Public Participation: The Use of Strategic Litigation to Silence Political Expression* (Waterloo, ON: Wilfrid Laurier University Press, 2014).

25 Macfarlane, "How a Good Idea Became a Bad Idea."

26 Sara Ahmed, *Complaint!* (Durham, NC: Duke University Press, 2021), 99.

27 Normand Glaude, *Report of the Cornwall Inquiry* (Toronto: Ontario Attorney General, 2009), https://www.attorneygeneral.jus.gov.on.ca/inquiries/cornwall/en/index.htm.
28 Glaude, *Report of the Cornwall Inquiry*.
29 Glaude, *Report of the Cornwall Inquiry*.
30 Glaude, *Report of the Cornwall Inquiry*.
31 Glaude, *Report of the Cornwall Inquiry*, 387.
32 Glaude, *Report of the Cornwall Inquiry*, 388.
33 Aidan Macnab, "CBA Adopts Resolutions on NDAs and Intersectional Judicial Data Collection at Annual Meeting," *Canadian Lawyer*, February 10, 2023, https://www.canadianlawyermag.com/resources/practice-management/cba-adopts-resolutions-on-ndas-and-intersectional-judicial-data-collection-at-annual-meeting/373623.
34 Bonnie Robichaud released a book detailing her legal case and the "secret agreement." See Bonnie Robichaud, *It Should Be Easy to Fix* (Toronto: Between the Lines, 2022).
35 When I shared my research findings with Laura nearly two years after this interview, she told me that while they did not reach a settlement agreement, the organization needed to declare bankruptcy and cited her complaint and the legal costs as a key reason for the bankruptcy.
36 Glaude, *Report of the Cornwall Inquiry*.
37 *WIC Radio Ltd v Simpson*, 2008 SCC 40, [2008] 2 SCR 420, para 15, http://canlii.ca/t/1z46d.
38 Bailey Gerrits, "Who Is Responsible? Explaining How Contemporary Canadian Newspapers Frame Domestic Violence" (PhD diss., Queen's University, 2019).
39 Gerrits, "Who Is Responsible?," 123.
40 Gerrits, "Who Is Responsible?," 123.
41 Canadian Press, "CTV Serves Statement of Defence to Patrick Brown in Defamation Lawsuit," *CBC News*, July 7, 2018, https://www.cbc.ca/news/canada/toronto/ctv-patrick-brown-defamation-allegations-1.4738096.
42 Joseph Brean, "Shamed by #MeToo Allegations, Canadian Poet Sues His Accusers, and Media Who Reported Story," *National Post*, July 12, 2018, https://nationalpost.com/news/canada/shamed-by-metoo-allegations-canadian-poet-sues-his-accusers-and-media-who-reported-story.
43 Brean, "Shamed by #MeToo Allegations."
44 Alicia Elliott, "How a Canadian Law Is Silencing Victims of Gender-Based Violence," *Flare*, December 6, 2018, https://www.flare.com/news/canadian-libel-law/, accessed January 5, 2019. Right before this article was published, Alicia Elliott was sued by Steven Galloway. The notice of civil claim cites four tweets written by Elliott as being defamatory. Likely for legal reasons, Elliott does not address the lawsuit initiated by Galloway in this piece.

45 Elliott, "How a Canadian Law Is Silencing Victims."
46 Elliott, "How a Canadian Law Is Silencing Victims."
47 Elliott, "How a Canadian Law Is Silencing Victims."
48 Marilou McPhedran, interview with author, March 20, 2019.
49 McPhedran, interview.
50 McPhedran, interview.

Chapter 4: Campus Sexual Violence

1 Jackie Hong, "Fired Yukon College Instructor Sues Student over Sex Assault Allegations," *Yukon News,* October 26, 2018, https://www.yukon-news.com/news/fired-yukon-college-instructor-sues-student-over-sex-assault-allegations/; and Terri Theodore, "Novelist Steven Galloway Files Defamation Suit over Sexual Assault Allegations," *Toronto Star,* October 30, 2018, https://www.thestar.com/entertainment/2018/10/30/novelist-steven-galloway-files-defamation-suit-over-sexual-assault-allegations.html.
2 Kelsey Litwin, "McGill University Professor Sues Colleague, Former Student for $600,000," *Montreal Gazette,* July 5, 2018, https://montrealgazette.com/news/local-news/mcgill-university-professor-sues-former-student-colleague-for-600000.
3 Julie Macfarlane, *Going Public: A Survivor's Journey from Grief to Action* (Toronto: Between the Lines, 2020).
4 Sara Ahmed, *Complaint!* (Durham, NC: Duke University Press, 2021).
5 Rob Lurie, "McGill Student Sues School, Student Paper and Others over Sexual Assault Allegation," *CTV News,* November 19, 2020, https://montreal.ctvnews.ca/mcgill-student-sues-school-student-paper-and-others-over-sexual-assault-allegation-1.5197206.
6 Elizabeth Quinlan, Andrea Quinlan, Curtis Fogel, and Gail Taylor, eds., *Sexual Violence at Canadian Universities: Activism, Institutional Responses, and Strategies for Change* (Waterloo, ON: Wilfrid Laurier University Press, 2017).
7 Mary P. Koss, Christine A. Gidycz, and Nadine Wisniewski, "The Scope of Rape: Incidence and Prevalence of Sexual Aggression and Victimization in a National Sample of Higher Education Students," *Journal of Consulting and Clinical Psychology* 55, 2 (1987): 162–70, https://doi.org/10.1037/0022-006X.55.2.162; Walter S. DeKeseredy and Martin D. Schwartz, *Woman Abuse on Campus: Results from the Canadian National Survey,* Sage Series on Violence against Women, vol. 5 (Thousand Oaks, CA: Sage, 1998); and Chilly Collective, *Breaking Anonymity: The Chilly Climate for Women Faculty* (Waterloo, ON: Wilfrid Laurier University Press, 1995).
8 Canadian Press, "UBC Alumna Files Human Rights Complaint over Sexual Assault Response," *CBC News,* March 31, 2016, https://www.cbc.ca/news/canada/british-columbia/ubc-aluma-human-rights-complaint-filed-1.3515572; Kristy Hoffman, "York

University's Sexual Assault Policy Sparks Human Rights Complaint," *Globe and Mail,* June 30, 2015, https://www.theglobeandmail.com/news/national/education/york-universitys-sexual-assault-policy-sparks-human-rights-complaint/article25194134/; Laura Kane, "UBC Denies Mishandling Sex Assault Complaints in Response to Human Rights Battle," *CBC News,* November 20, 2017, https://www.cbc.ca/news/canada/british-columbia/ubc-sexual-assault-human-rights-complaints-1.4411398; and Lisa Xing, "'It Was Horrifying': Former Student Says University Revictimized Her during Sexual Assault Investigation," *CBC News,* September 11, 2017, https://www.cbc.ca/news/canada/toronto/university-sexual-assault-investigation-leads-to-human-rights-complaint-1.4275622.

9   See Ahmed, *Complaint!*; Mandi Gray, Laura Pin, and Annelies Cooper, "Curate Consultation and the Illusion of Inclusion in York University's Sexual Assault Policy Making Process," in *Dis/Consent: Perspectives on Sexual Consent and Sexual Violence,* ed. KellyAnne Malinen (Halifax: Fernwood, 2019), 32–42.
10 Leila Whitley and Tiffany Page, "Sexism at the Centre: Locating the Problem of Sexual Harassment," *New Formations* 86 (Winter 2015): 34–53, https://doi.org/10.3898/NEWF.86.02.2015.
11 Canadian Press, "Sex-Harassment Charge Touches Off Libel Action," *Globe and Mail,* March 26, 1981; Canadian Press, "Carleton Accusers Face Libel Counts," *Globe and Mail,* June 17, 1981.
12 Canadian Press, "Carleton Accusers Face Libel Counts."
13 Chilly Collective, *Breaking Anonymity*.
14 Chilly Collective, *Breaking Anonymity,* 7.
15 Interview with Constance Backhouse, March 19, 2019.
16 Interview with Constance Backhouse, March 19, 2019.
17 Marta Burczycka, "Students' Experiences of Unwanted Sexualized Behaviours and Sexual Assault at Postsecondary Schools in the Canadian Provinces, 2019," *Juristat,* September 14, 2019, Canadian Centre for Justice and Community Safety Statistics, Statistics Canada, https://www150.statcan.gc.ca/n1/pub/85-002-x/2020001/article/00005-eng.htm.
18 Burczycka, "Students' Experiences of Unwanted Sexualized Behaviours."
19 Burczycka, "Students' Experiences of Unwanted Sexualized Behaviours."
20 Burczycka, "Students' Experiences of Unwanted Sexualized Behaviours."
21 Gray, Pin, and Cooper, "Curate Consultation"; Caitlin Salvino, Kelsey Gilchrist, and Jade Cooligan-Pang, *Our Turn: A National Student-Led Action Plan to End Campus Sexual Violence* (Montreal: Student's Society of McGill University, 2017), https://static1.squarespace.com/static/5bc4e7bcf4755a6e42b00495/t/5f107ac2b2f3cd2f9b6fe449/1594915540325/our_turn_action_plan_en_2020-05-26.pdf; Quinlan et al., *Sexual Violence at Canadian Universities;* Emma Smith, "Every N.S. University to

Receive Bystander Training to Address Sexual Violence," *CBC News,* March 6, 2020, https://www.cbc.ca/news/canada/nova-scotia/bystander-training-antigonish-women-s-centre-university-college-campus-1.5489077; and Anna-Lee Straatman, "Bystander Sexual Violence Education Programs for High School, College and University Students," LearningNetwork Brief 09, Learning Network, Centre for Research and Education on Violence Against Women and Children, London, Ontario, 2013, http://www.vawlearningnetwork.ca/our-work/briefs/briefpdfs/LB-09.pdf.

22 F. Khan, C.J. Rowe, and R. Bidgood, *Courage to Act: Developing a National Framework to Address and Prevent Gender-Based Violence at Post-Secondary Institutions in Canada* (Toronto: Possibility Seeds, 2019), 7, https://static1.squarespace.com/static/5d482d9fd8b74f0001c02192/t/62ac86307f9bb400023b8598/1655473740770/Courage+to+Act+Report+2022.pdf.

23 It's important to note that during the early 1990s, when the issue of campus sexual harassment was first being addressed, many universities had dedicated sexual harassment centres. By the 2000s, many of these centres were rebranded under the broader framework of human rights.

24 Emily M. Colpitts, "'Not Even Close to Enough': Sexual Violence, Intersectionality, and the Neoliberal University," *Gender and Education* 34, 2 (2021): 1–16, https://doi.org/10.1080/09540253.2021.1924362; and Gray, Pin, and Cooper, "Curate Consultation."

25 Colpitts, "Not Even Close to Enough," 1–16.

26 Colpitts, "'Not Even Close to Enough,'" 4.

27 Karen Busby, "Accountability Mechanisms in University Sexual Violence Policies," *Canadian Yearbook of Human Rights, 2016/2018* (Ottawa: Human Rights Research and Education Centre, University of Ottawa, 2019), 49–58.

28 Whitley and Page, "Sexism at the Centre."

29 Fuyuki Kurasawa, "Which Barbarians at the Gates? From the Culture Wars to Market Orthodoxy in the North American Academy," *Canadian Review of Sociology/Revue Canadienne de Sociologie* 39, 3 (2008): 323–47, https://doi.org/10.1111/j.1755-618X.2002.tb00623.x.

30 Alison Phipps, "Reckoning Up: Sexual Harassment and Violence in the Neoliberal University," *Gender and Education* 32, 2 (2020): 227–43, https://doi.org/10.1080/09540253.2018.1482413.

31 Phipps, "Reckoning Up."

32 Emily M. Colpitts, "Addressing Sexual Violence at Ontario Universities in the Context of Rising Anti-feminist Backlash," *Atlantis* 41, 1 (2020): 45–58; Mandi Gray and Laura Pin, "'I Would like It If Some of Our Tuition Went to Providing Pepper Spray for Students': University Branding, Securitization and Campus Sexual Assault at a Canadian University," *Annual Review of Interdisciplinary Justice Studies* 6 (2017): 86–110; and Julie Gregory, "University Branding via Securitization," *TOPIA: Canadian*

Journal of Cultural Studies 28 (Fall 2012): 65–86, https://doi.org/10.3138/topia.28.65; and Phipps, "Reckoning Up."
33 Phipps, "Reckoning Up."
34 Julie Macfarlane, "How a Good Idea Became a Bad Idea: Universities and the Use of Non-disclosure Agreements in Terminations for Sexual Misconduct," *Cardozo Journal of Conflict Resolution* 21 (2020): 361–79; and Phipps, "Reckoning Up."
35 Phipps, "Reckoning Up."
36 Phipps, "Reckoning Up."
37 Gregory, "University Branding via Securitization."
38 Ahmed, *Complaint!*, 125.
39 In 2021, two students at this university published a call to action because of the lack of sexual violence resources available. The university responded that there would be a policy review and pointed to the sexual assault policy and the centre as evidence that the university takes sexual violence seriously. Sara Ahmed notes that universities tend to use their own policies as evidence of action, regardless of how complicated or challenging these policies are to access, a practice she refers to as "strategic inefficiency": Ahmed, *Complaint!*, 91.
40 Jasmine Tucker and Jennifer Mondino, *Coming Forward: Key Trends and Data from the TIME'S UP Legal Defense Fund* (Washington, DC: TIME'S UP/National Women's Law Centre, 2020), 12, https://nwlc.org/wp-content/uploads/2020/10/NWLC-Intake-Report_FINAL_2020-10-13.pdf.
41 Jennifer Freyd, "Violations of Power, Adaptive Blindness and Betrayal Trauma Theory," *Feminist Psychology* 7, 1 (1997): 22–32.
42 *Macfarlane v Canadian Universities Reciprocal Insurance Exchange*, [2019] OJ No 4185, 2019 ONSC 4631.
43 Gerster, "Trinidad Court."
44 Julie Macfarlane, interview with author, March 2019. Macfarlane recently initiated a campaign to ban the use of nondisclosure agreements in matters of sexual violence as a concrete step that institutions should take to stop protecting perpetrators of sexual violence. In 2023, Senator Marilou McPhedran in collaboration with Macfarlane drafted a Senate bill that aims to prevent the federal government from using NDAs to cover up misconduct in the civil service. See CBC, "NDAs Aimed to Protect Trade Secrets. Now They're Often Hiding Bad Behaviour, Says Prof," May 26, 2023, https://www.cbc.ca/radio/day6/julie-macfarlane-ndas-senate-1.6855610; Ashley Burke, "New Bill before the Senate Would Crack Down on Non-Disclosure Agreements," May 9, 2023, https://www.cbc.ca/news/politics/new-bill-introduced-senate-limit-use-non-disclosure-agreements-1.6837422.
45 Mark Gollom, "Law Professor Accuses University of Windsor of Hiding Documents in Defamation Case," *CBC News*, September 10, 2020, https://www.cbc.ca/news/

julie-macfarlane-university-windsor-defamation-documents-1.5717114. As of November 2021, Julie Macfarlane had dropped the lawsuit against the University of Windsor. Julie Macfarlane, interview with author, November 2021.

Chapter 5: Is Anti-SLAPP Legislation the Answer?

1 Penelope Canan and George Pring, "Strategic Lawsuits against Public Participation," *Social Problems* 35, 5 (1988): 506.
2 Canan and Pring, "Strategic Lawsuits."
3 *1704604 Ontario Limited v Pointes Protection Association et al*, 2020 SCC 22 [*1704604*], https://canlii.ca/t/j9kjz.
4 Nick Phillips and Ryan Pumpian, "A Constitutional Counterpunch to Georgia's Anti-SLAPP Statute," *Mercer Law Review* 69, 2 (2018): 407; and Byron M. Sheldrick, *Blocking Public Participation: The Use of Strategic Litigation to Silence Political Expression* (Waterloo, ON: Wilfrid Laurier University Press, 2014).
5 Sheldrick, *Blocking Public Participation*.
6 This chapter does not include the Quebec legislation because of the language barrier. For literature on anti-SLAPP protections in Quebec, see Normand Landry, "From the Streets to the Courtroom: The Legacies of Quebec's Anti-SLAPP Movement," *Review of European Community and International Environmental Law* 19, 1 (2014): 58–69.
7 Barbra Schlifer Commemorative Clinic, "Factum of the Intervener Barbra Schlifer Commemorative Clinic," SCC, 2019, file 38374, https://www.scc-csc.ca/WebDocuments-DocumentsWeb/38374/FM120_Intervener_Barbra-Schlifer-Commemorative-Clinic.pdf; BC Coalition, "Factum of the Interveners, West Coast Legal Education and Action Fund, Atira Women's Resource Society, B.W.S.S. Battered Women's Support Services Association, Women Against Violence Against Women Rape Crisis Centre," SCC, 2019, file 38374, https://www.scc-csc.ca/WebDocuments-DocumentsWeb/38374/FM130_Interveners_West-Coast-Legal-Education-and-Action-Fund-et-al.pdf; Bruce E.H. Johnson and Antoinette Bonsignore, "Protect #MeToo Victims from Retaliatory Lawsuits," *Seattle Times*, January 23, 2018, https://www.seattletimes.com/opinion/protect-metoo-victims-from-retaliatory-lawsuits/; and Alyssa R. Leader, "SLAPP in the Face of Free Speech: Protecting Survivors' Rights to Speak Up in the Me Too Era," *First Amendment Law Review* 17, 3 (2019): 441–76.
8 Ontario, Legislative Assembly, Standing Committee on Justice Policy, "Protection of Public Participation Act, 2015," in *Official Report of Debates (Hansard)*, No JP-8 (September 24, 2015), JP83-86, JP108-110, https://www.ola.org/en/legislative-business/committees/justice-policy/parliament-41/transcripts/committee-transcript-2015-sep-24#P55_3045.
9 Ontario, "Protection of Public Participation Act," 84.

10 Ontario, "Protection of Public Participation Act," 108.
11 *Protection of Public Participation Act,* SO, 2015, c 23, s 137.1(1).
12 *Courts of Justice Act,* RSO, 1990, s 137; and *Protection of Public Participation Act,* SBC, 2019, c 3. The only major difference between the two acts is that the Ontario act states that the application must be heard within sixty days, whereas the British Columbia act states that the "application must be heard as soon as practicable" (s 9(3)).
13 *1704604.*
14 *1704604,* para 103.
15 *1704604,* para 28, emphasis added.
16 *Bent v Platnick,* 2020 SCC 23, para 96 [*Bent*], https://www.canlii.org/en/ca/scc/doc/2020/2020scc23/2020scc23.html.
17 *Bent,* para 139.
18 *1704604,* para 81.
19 *Bent,* para 140.
20 *Bent,* para 140.
21 BC Coalition, "Factum of the Interveners."
22 BC Coalition, "Factum of the Interveners," para 4.
23 BC Coalition, "Factum of the Interveners," para 14.
24 Barbra Schlifer Commemorative Clinic, "Factum."
25 See *Lyncaster v Metro Vancouver Kink Society,* 2019 BCSC 2207 [*Lyncaster*], http://canlii.ca/t/j481r; and *Smith v Nagy,* 2021 ONSC 4265, para 48, https://canlii.ca/t/jgfnx; and *Bullard v Rogers Media Inc,* 2020 ONSC 3084 [*Bullard*], http://canlii.ca/t/j7t0f.
26 *Rizvee v Newman,* 2017 ONSC 4024, http://canlii.ca/t/h4npx.
27 *Galloway v A.B.,* 2021 BCSC 2344. At the time of writing, this decision is being appealed by both the plaintiff and several defendants, including myself. Therefore, I have excluded this decision from the analysis.
28 Tim Whitnell, "Second Lawsuit against Milton Journalist Abandoned in Court," *InsideHalton.com,* November 2, 2018, https://www.insidehalton.com/news-story/9003925-second-lawsuit-against-milton-journalist-abandoned-in-106court/.
29 *Rizvee v Newman,* para 40. The use of peace bonds in common law dates to thirteenth-century England. The intention is to govern minor disputes between individuals. The legal test for a peace bond is the determination of "reasonable fear." To date, there is little research on peace bonds in Canada. See Mark D. Doerksen, "Fighting Fear with Fear: Governmental Criminology of Peace Bonds" (master's thesis, University of Ottawa, 2013), https://ruor.uottawa.ca/bitstream/10393/24224/1/Doerksen_Mark_2013_thesis.pdf.
30 *Rizvee v Newman,* para 47.

31 The refusal of the Crown to move forward with the peace bond is not an isolated incident but rather represents the systemic failure of the courts to adequately recognize and respond to gendered violence. Feminist antiviolence advocates have long criticized the courts for making it incredibly difficult for women to get protection orders. See Katie Dangerfield, "'A Piece of Paper That Did Nothing': Advocates Say Protection Orders Are Failing Women in Canada," *Global News,* June 6, 2019, https://globalnews.ca/news/3965001/protection-orders-canada-failing-women/.
32 *Rizvee v Newman,* para 135.
33 Whitnell, "Second Lawsuit."
34 *Ng v C.G.,* 2020 ONSC 6825. The tort of malicious prosecution is intended to protect individuals from baseless criminal prosecutions. For a malicious prosecution claim to be successful, the plaintiff is required to prove that the defendant initiated criminal proceedings against the plaintiff, that the criminal proceedings terminated in the plaintiff's favour, that there is no reasonable and probable cause for the proceedings, that there was malice on the part of the defendant, and that the plaintiff sustained damages. Unlike other torts where motive is not usually taken into consideration, the prosecution must be motivated by malice. See Philip H. Osborne, *The Law of Torts,* 5th ed., Essentials of Canadian Law (Toronto: Irwin Law, 2015).
35 *Ng v C.G.,* para 59.
36 *Ng v C.G.,* para 65.
37 *Mazhar v Farooqi,* 2020 ONSC 3490, https://canlii.ca/t/j86hf.
38 *Mazhar v Farooqi,* para 81.
39 Sara Blaze, "Open Letter to Lord Braven from the MVK Board," Facebook, *MVK: Metro Vancouver Kink Facebook Page,* July 12, 2017, https://www.facebook.com/groups/6949777007/permalink/10155458993592008/, accessed June 15, 2022.
40 Jennifer Saltman, "Defamation Suit against Metro Vancouver Kink Society to Proceed," *Vancouver Sun,* December 23, 2019, https://vancouversun.com/news/local-news/defamation-suit-against-metro-vancouver-kink-society-to-proceed.
41 Blaze, "Open Letter."
42 Saltman, "Defamation Suit against Metro Vancouver Kink Society."
43 *Lyncaster,* para 27.
44 *Lyncaster,* para 62.
45 *Lyncaster,* para 62.
46 For a discussion of the decision to report sexual violence that occurs in the context of BDSM, see Noam Haviv, "Reporting Sexual Assaults to the Police: The Israeli BDSM Community," *Sexuality Research and Social Policy* 13, 3 (2016): 276–87, https://doi.org/10.1007/s13178-016-0222-4.
47 See Chanelle Gallant and Andrea Zanin, "The Bogus BDSM Defence: The Manipulation of Kink as Consent to Assault," in *Dis/Consent: Perspectives on Sexual*

Consent and Sexual Violence, ed. KelleyAnne Malinen (Halifax: Fernwood, 2019), 32–42.
48 *Smith v Nagy,* para 48.
49 *Smith v Nagy,* para 54.
50 *Bullard,* para 1.
51 *Bullard,* para 102.
52 *Bullard,* para 103.
53 *Courts of Justice Act,* RSO, 1990, s 137.2(5), https://www.ontario.ca/laws/statute/s15023.
54 Because of the private nature of these cross-examinations, it is challenging to study the types of questions that silence breakers are subjected to. I have reviewed several transcripts of cross-examinations in anti-SLAPP motions but am unable to report on their contents because of confidentiality. For a nuanced discussion on the tactics of lawyers in criminal sexual assault trials, see Elaine Craig, *Putting Trials on Trial: Sexual Assault and the Failure of the Legal Profession* (Montreal/Kingston: McGill-Queen's University Press, 2018); and Daniel Tanovich, "'Whack' No More: Infusing Equality into the Ethics of Defence Lawyering in Sexual Assault Cases," *Ottawa Law Review* 45, 3 (2015): 495–525.
55 David Ward, "In Her Words: Recognizing and Preventing Abusive Litigation against Domestic Violence Survivors," *Seattle Journal for Social Justice* 14, 2 (2016): 429–64.
56 I am a defendant in the Galloway case, but I was not a party to this motion. As a result of the motion, some of my personal email correspondence with A.B. were produced by her.
57 Stephanie R. Larson, "Survivors, Liars, and Unfit Minds: Rhetorical Impossibility and Rape Trauma Disclosure," *Hypatia* 33, 4 (2018): 681.
58 *Galloway v A.B.,* 2020 BCCA 106, paras 67–68.
59 Lise Gotell, "When Privacy Is Not Enough: Sexual Assault Complainants, Sexual History Evidence and the Disclosure of Personal Records," *Alberta Law Review* 43, 3 (2006): 769.
60 Gotell, "When Privacy Is Not Enough," 769.
61 Hilary Young, "Anti-SLAPP's Unintended Consequences," *Canadian Lawyer,* October 15, 2021, https://www.canadianlawyermag.com/news/opinion/anti-slapps-unintended-consequences/360790.

Conclusion

1 Penelope Canan and George Pring, "Strategic Lawsuits against Public Participation," *Social Problems* 35, 5 (1988): 509–19.
2 Statistics Canada, Table 35-10-0112-01, "Civil Court Cases, by Level of Court and Type of Case, Canada and Selected Provinces and Territories," https://doi.org/10.25318/3510011201-eng.

3 Michele R. Decker, Charvonne N. Holliday, Zaynab Hameeduddin, Roma Shah, Janice Miller, Joyce Dantler, and Leigh Goodmark, "'You Do Not Think of Me as a Human Being': Race and Gender Inequities Intersect to Discourage Police Reporting of Violence against Women," *Journal of Urban Health* 96, 5 (2019): 772–83, https://doi.org/10.1007/s11524-019-00359-z; and Jodie Murphy-Oikonen, Lori Chambers, Karen McQueen, Alexa Hiebert, and Ainsley Miller, "Sexual Assault: Indigenous Women's Experiences of Not Being Believed by the Police," *Violence against Women* 28, 5 (2021): 1035–76, https://doi.org/10.1177/10778012211013903.
4 *Caron v A.*, 2015 BCCA 47, http://canlii.ca/t/gg863.
5 *Whitfield v Whitfield*, 2016 ONCA 581, http://canlii.ca/t/gsp2p; *Vanderkooy v Vanderkooy et al*, 2013 ONSC 4796, para 215, http://canlii.ca/t/g04cb; *Smith v Nagy*, 2021 ONSC 4265, para 48, https://canlii.ca/t/jgfnx; and *Lyncaster v Metro Vancouver Kink Society*, 2019 BCSC 2207, https://canlii.ca/t/jgfnx.
6 Karen Busby, "Accountability Mechanisms in University Sexual Violence Policies," *Canadian Yearbook of Human Rights, 2016/2018* (Ottawa: Human Rights Research and Education Centre, University of Ottawa, 2019), 49–58.
7 Jennifer Freyd, "Violations of Power, Adaptive Blindness and Betrayal Trauma Theory," *Feminist Psychology* 7, 1 (1997): 22–32.
8 Freyd, "Violations of Power."
9 Barbra Schlifer Commemorative Clinic, "Factum of the Intervener Barbra Schlifer Commemorative Clinic," SCC, 2019, file 38374, https://www.scc-csc.ca/WebDocuments-DocumentsWeb/38374/FM120_Intervener_Barbra-Schlifer-Commemorative-Clinic.pdf; Bruce E.H. Johnson and Antoinette Bonsignore, "Protect #MeToo Victims from Retaliatory Lawsuits," *Seattle Times*, January 23, 2018, https://www.seattletimes.com/opinion/protect-metoo-victims-from-retaliatory-lawsuits/; and Alyssa R. Leader, "SLAPP in the Face of Free Speech: Protecting Survivors' Rights to Speak Up in the Me Too Era," *First Amendment Law Review* 17, 3 (2019): 441–76.
10 Marta Burczycka, "Students' Experiences of Unwanted Sexualized Behaviours and Sexual Assault at Postsecondary Schools in the Canadian Provinces, 2019," *Juristat*, September 14, 2019, Canadian Centre for Justice and Community Safety Statistics, Statistics Canada, https://www150.statcan.gc.ca/n1/pub/85-002-x/2020001/article/00005-eng.htm; Shana Conroy and Adam Cotter, "Self-Reported Sexual Assault in Canada," Statistics Canada, July 11, 2017, https://www150.statcan.gc.ca/n1/pub/85-002-x/2017001/article/14842-eng.htm; Holly Johnson, "Why Doesn't She Just Report It? Apprehensions and Contradictions for Women Who Report Sexual Violence to the Police," *Canadian Journal of Women and the Law* 29, 36 (2017): 36–59.
11 See Shawn Meghan Burn, "A Situational Model of Sexual Assault Prevention through Bystander Intervention," *Sex Roles* 60, 11–12 (2009): 779–92, https://doi.org/10.1007/s11199-008-9581-5; Danielle Labhardt, Emma Holdsworth, Sarah Brown, and

Douglas Howat, "You See but You Do Not Observe: A Review of Bystander Intervention and Sexual Assault on University Campuses," *Aggression and Violent Behavior* 35 (July 2017): 13–25, https://doi.org/10.1016/j.avb.2017.05.005.

12 Kristin Bumiller, *In an Abusive State: How Neoliberalism Appropriated the Feminist Movement against Sexual Violence* (Durham, NC: Duke University Press, 2008).

13 For example, in 2001, British Columbia enacted anti-SLAPP legislation, which was quickly repealed after an election. See Michaelin Scott and Chris Tollefson, "Strategic Lawsuits against Public Participation: The British Columbia Experience," *Review of European, Comparative and International Environmental Law* 19, 1 (2010): 45–57.

14 *Caron v A*.

15 *Westcott v Westcott*, [2008] EWCA Civ 818, [2009] QB 407, [2009] 2 WLR 838, [2009] EMLR 2, [2009] 1 All ER 727, para 36, https://www.bailii.org/ew/cases/EWCA/Civ/2008/818.html.

Selected Bibliography

Case Law

Bent v Platnick, 2020 SCC 23, https://www.canlii.org/en/ca/scc/doc/2020/2020scc23/2020scc23.html

Bullard v Rogers Media Inc, 2020 ONSC 3084, http://canlii.ca/t/j7t0f

Canadian Newspapers Co v Canada (Attorney General), [1988] 2 SCR 122, 1988 SCC 52, http://canlii.ca/t/1ftdc

Caron v A., 2015 BCCA 47, http://canlii.ca/t/gg863

Franchuk v Schick, 2014 ABQB 249, http://canlii.ca/t/g7rt9

Galloway v A.B., 2019 BCSC 395, http://canlii.ca/t/hznmr

Galloway v A.B., 2019 BCSC 1417, http://canlii.ca/t/j23nd

Galloway v A.B., 2020 BCCA 106, http://canlii.ca/t/j6chr

Hill v Church of Scientology of Toronto, 1995 SCC 59, [1995] 2 SCR 1130, http://canlii.ca/t/1frgn

Lyncaster v Metro Vancouver Kink Society, 2019 BCSC 2207, http://canlii.ca/t/j48lr

Macfarlane v Canadian Universities Reciprocal Insurance Exchange, 2019 ONSC 4631, http://canlii.ca/t/j1z8q

Mainstream Canada v Staniford, 2013 BCCA 341, http://canlii.ca/t/fzqsx

Ng v C.G., 2020 ONSC 6825 (unreported decision)

Rizvee v Newman, 2017 ONSC 4024, http://canlii.ca/t/h4npx

Smith v Nagy, 2021 ONSC 4265, https://canlii.ca/t/jgfnx

Stuart v Doe, 2019 YKSC 53, http://canlii.ca/t/j34c1

Vanderkooy v Vanderkooy et al, 2013 ONSC 4796, http://canlii.ca/t/g04cb

Westcott v Westcott [2008] EWCA Civ 818, [2009] QB 407, [2009] 2 WLR 838, [2009] EMLR 2, [2009] 1 All ER 727, https://www.bailii.org/ew/cases/EWCA/Civ/2008/818.html

Whitfield v Whitfield, 2014 ONSC 2745, http://canlii.ca/t/g6s8v
Whitfield v Whitfield, 2016 ONCA 581, http://canlii.ca/t/gsp2p
WIC Radio Ltd v Simpson, 2008 SCC 40, [2008] 2 SCR 420, http://canlii.ca/t/1z46d

Legislation

Courts of Justice Act, RSO, 1990, s 137
Limitations Act, SO 2002, c 24, Schedule B
Protection of Public Participation Act, SBC, 2019, c 3
Protection of Public Participation Act, SO, 2015, c 23
Rules of Civil Procedure, RRO 1990, Reg 194

Other Sources

Ahmed, Sara. *Complaint!* Durham, NC: Duke University Press, 2021.
Borden, Diane L. "Patterns of Harm: An Analysis of Gender and Defamation." *Communication Law and Policy* 2, 1 (1997): 105–41. https://doi.org/10.1080/10811689709368620.
–. "Reputational Assault: A Critical and Historical Analysis of Gender and the Law of Defamation." *Journalism and Mass Communication Quarterly* 75, 1 (1998): 98–111. https://doi.org/10.1177/107769909807500111.
Busby, Karen. "Accountability Mechanisms in University Sexual Violence Policies." *Canadian Yearbook of Human Rights, 2016/2018*, 49–58. Ottawa: Human Rights Research and Education Centre, 2019.
Canan, Penelope, and George W. Pring. "Strategic Lawsuits Against Public Participation." *Social Problems* 35, 5 (1988): 506–19. https://doi.org/10.2307/800612.
Colpitts, Emily M. "'Not Even Close to Enough': Sexual Violence, Intersectionality, and the Neoliberal University." *Gender and Education* 34, 2 (2021): 1–16. https://doi.org/10.1080/09540253.2021.1924362.
Craig, Elaine. *Putting Trials on Trial: Sexual Assault and the Failure of the Legal Profession*. Montreal/Kingston: McGill-Queen's University Press, 2018.
Danay, Robert. "The Medium Is Not the Message: Reconciling Reputation and Free Expression in Cases of Internet Defamation." *McGill Law Journal* 56, 1 (2010): 1–35.
Delaet, Debra, and Elizabeth Mills. "Discursive Silence as a Global Response to Sexual Violence: From Title IX to Truth Commissions." *Global Society* 32, 4 (2018): 496–519.
Duke, Katie. "Calling a Racist a Racist: A Case for Reforming the Tort of Defamation." *Windsor Review of Legal and Social Issues* 37, 70 (2016): 70–97.
Freyd, Jennifer. "Violations of Power, Adaptive Blindness and Betrayal Trauma Theory." *Feminist Psychology* 7, 1 (1997): 22–32.

Gilmore, Leigh. *Tainted Witness: Why We Doubt What Women Say about Their Lives*. New York: Columbia University Press, 2017.

Lisak, David, Lori Gardinier, Sarah C. Nicksa, and Ashley M. Cote. "False Allegations of Sexual Assault: An Analysis of Ten Years of Reported Cases." *Violence against Women* 16, 12 (2010): 1318–34. https://doi.org/10.1177/1077801210387747.

Macfarlane, Julie. "How a Good Idea Became a Bad Idea: Universities and the Use of Non-disclosure Agreements in Terminations for Sexual Misconduct." *Cardozo Journal of Conflict Resolution* 21 (2020): 361–79.

Osborne, Philip H. *The Law of Torts*. 5th ed. Essentials of Canadian Law. Toronto: Irwin Law, 2015.

Post, Robert C. "The Social Foundations of Defamation Law: Reputation and the Constitution." *California Law Review* 74, 3 (1986): 691–742.

Pruitt, Lisa R. "'On the Chastity of Women All Property in the World Depends': Injury from Sexual Slander in the Nineteenth Century." *Indiana Law Journal* 78, 3 (2003): 965–1018.

Sheldrick, Byron M. *Blocking Public Participation: The Use of Strategic Litigation to Silence Political Expression*. Waterloo, ON: Wilfrid Laurier University Press, 2014.

Skolnick, Jerome H. "Foreword: The Sociological Tort of Defamation." *California Law Review* 74, 3 (1986): 677–89.

Walker, Janet Elizabeth, and Lorne Mitchell Sossin. *Civil Litigation*. Essentials of Canadian Law. Toronto: Irwin Law, 2010.

Ward, David. "In Her Words: Recognizing and Preventing Abusive Litigation against Domestic Violence Survivors." *Seattle Journal for Social Justice* 14, 2 (2016): 429–64.

Young, Hilary. "The Canadian Defamation Action: An Empirical Study." *Canadian Bar Review* 95, 3 (2017): 591–630.

Index

Note: "DARVO" stands for Deny, Attack, Reverse Victim and Offender; "NDA," for non-disclosure agreements; "SLAPPs," for strategic lawsuits against public participation

absolute privilege. *See* privilege
Ahmed, Sara, 71, 80, 85
Ali (research participant), 22, 89, 91, 132*n*6
anti-SLAPP legislation: British Columbia legislation, 96–97; cost of motion, 109–10; Ontario legislation, 95–97; Quebec legislation, 95, 148*n*6; Supreme Court of Canada, 94, 97–98. *See also* Courts of Justice Act s.137 (ON); Protection of Public Participation Act (BC)
anti-violence activism, 80, 85, 86, 124
Atwood, Margaret, viii

Backhouse, Constance, 8, 11, 30, 81
Balfour, Gillian, 41
Barbra Schlifer Commemorative Clinic, 44, 98
betrayal trauma. *See* institutional betrayal
Birenbaum, Joanna, vii, 44–45, 122

Blasey Ford, Christine, 8
Boesveld, Sarah, 105
Borden, Diane, 47
Bourke, Joanna, vi
Bullard v Rogers Media Inc, 105
Busby, Karen, 82
Buzzfeed News, 77
bystanders: fear of lawsuits, 69, 75; health impacts of bystanders who were sued, 63; privilege (social), 70, 91, 123; reputational harm, 93; sued, 15; support of, 120; supporting survivors, 87, 91–92; university campaigns, 115; use of anti-SLAPP legislation, 99

Cadieux-Shaw, Lillian, 10
Camila (research participant), 64, 67–68
campus sexual violence: consequences of campus sexual violence, 63–64; faculty supporting students who

report sexual assault, 70, 87, 115, 120; formal reports, 114; policies, 80–83, 147n39; reports of faculty sexual assault, 38, 79, 83–84; securitization of campus, 84; statistics, 80–81; university branding, 79. *See also* university complaint processes

Canadian Bar Association (CBA), 71–72

Canadian Universities Reciprocal Insurance Exchange (CURIE), 89–90

carceral feminism, 121

Carleton University, 81

Caron v A, 53–54

Catherine (research participant): knowledge of legal system, 21; peace bond, 20; personal safety, 66; protection of future victims, 20; reporting to police, 114; retaining legal counsel, 23–24; served with lawsuit, 20, 132n6; settlement agreement, 64; social media posts, 21, 67, 114; suicidal ideation, 52; surveillance of online activity, 67; threat of countersuit, 52

cease-and-desist letters, 17–19, 24, 86, 101

Charlene (research participant), 87, 91, 115

childhood sexual violence, 71, 56–57, 65–66, 69. *See also* sexual assault; sexual violence

chilling effect. *See* silencing sexual violence discourse

chilly climate reports on gender discrimination, 81

Cornwall Public Inquiry (ON), 71, 74

costs of litigation: anti-SLAPP motions, 110, 142n20; cost of trial, 36; cost-benefit analysis before speaking or reporting, 69, 85, 115, 117; document production, 27, 108; factors for calculating costs in judgment, 37, 57; financial problems due to lawsuit, 4, 26, 36, 143n35; insurance coverage, 89; legal fees survey results, 35; loser pay rules, 36, 133n14; loss of career opportunities due to lawsuit, 4; pro bono legal representation, 24; recoup costs via countersuit, 26; silence breakers' legal fees, 70, 134n38. *See also* damages; lawyers

counterclaim for defamation, 56, 65

counterclaims for sexual violence: extensive document production, 28, 51; Amber Heard, 5; lawyer decision to take case, 26; legal advice in response to defamation lawsuit, 50; proof of sexual violence occurring, 50–51; silence breakers' perspectives, 52

Courts of Justice Act s.137 (ON), 96–97, 99, 105. *See also* anti-SLAPP legislation; SLAPPs

criminal legal system, 16

damages: ability to pay, 73; awarded, 5, 56, 47, 90; considerations for damages, 59–60; for countersuing, 26, 28, 50, 72; damages threatened, 18, 46, 55–57, 59, 80, 100, 103; in defamation law, 43; gender analysis, 48; pecuniary damages, 42, 60, 103; risk calculation, 36

Darlene (research participant), 73

DARVO (deny, attack, reverse victim and offender), 7, 11, 93, 118 defamation: criminal defamation, 49–50, 138n65; defences, 50–61, 121–23; fear of defamation lawsuit, 10, 69, 112, 116; as gendered, 47–49, 138n65; history of, 41–42, 45; legal definitions, 7, 42, 50, 97–98; libel, 42–43, 132n3, 139n72; provincial defamation acts, 139n72; replication of a criminal sexual assault trial, 110; serving lawsuit, viii, 14, 20, 22–24, 104, 132n6; slander, 42; as sociological, 43; statistics, 6, 23, 113; threats of defamation action, 7, 12, 18–19, 85, 118. *See also* cease-and-desist letters

Depp, Johnny, 5–6

Dickie, Hansel J.B.A., 31–34

discovery: document production, 26–29, 106–9; as invasive, 28, 31–34, 51; oral examination, 29–35; power imbalances, 29–30, 34–35, 39; trial by avalanche, 27. *See also* power dynamics

domestic violence, 5, 76, 105

Doolittle, Robyn, 9–10

Duke, Katie, 58–59

Elizabeth (research participant): campus sexual assault, 25; decision not to countersue, 52; lawsuit hindered healing, 63–64; report to police, 52–53; suicidal ideation, 52; thoughts on retaining counsel, 25–26

Elliott, Alicia, 77, 143n44

emotional distress: anti-therapeutic impacts of legal system, 62, 65, 119; betrayal trauma, 63, 90–91; bystanders, 63; due to cross-examination, 107; due to threat of lawsuit, 115; lawsuit impact on healing, 63–64, 73–74; research participants' experiences, 63–65; socially structured, 62. *See also* institutional betrayal; suicide

fair comment on a matter of public interest (defence): defence for media, 76; elements for courts to consider, 57–58; on social media, 58–59; Supreme Court of Canada, 58; use by silence breakers, 59

false allegations of sexual violence: Canadian media, 8; conflation with acquittals, 8; conflation with unfounded cases, 11; construction of men as the true victims, 6; construction of women as liars, 11; criminal charges, 3–4, 114; definition, 8–9; focus of public discourse, 7–8; public concern of growing problem, 8–9, 44–45; public retraction of allegations, 60; rare occurrence, 7, 44; reputational damage, 47; Supreme Court of Canada, 44–45

fear of being sued. *See* defamation

Franchuk v Schick, 55–56

Freeman Marshall, Patricia, 95–96

Freyd, Jennifer, 7, 118. *See also* DARVO

gag orders: causing emotional harm, 70–72, 74–75, 120; as censorship, 75, 117; definition, 70; lawyer perspectives, 73–74; pressure to agree, 71; silence breaker resistance to gag orders, 75; as violence, 70; in the workplace, 72

Galloway, Steven, viii–ix, 38; *Galloway v A.B.*, 38, 102, 109, 135*n*54
Gerrits, Bailey, 76
Gina (research participant), 86–87, 91, 93, 115
Globe and Mail: lawsuits against, 31, 77–78; unfounded cases series, 9
Gotell, Lise, 29, 109

health (physical), 62, 65–66, 74, 78, 119. *See also* emotional distress
Heard, Amber, 5
Hill v Church of Scientology of Toronto, 41–44, 54, 135*n*2
#HimToo, 8
hooks, bell, 12–13

Indigenous: access to justice for sexual violence, 114; media reports of violence against Indigenous women and children, 65–66, 77; reports of sexual assault to police, 10. *See also* police; reporting
institutional betrayal, 3, 63, 90, 119
intersectionality, 82

Janet (research participant), 69–70, 75
Jessica (research participant), 74, 117

Lalonde, Julie S., 84–85
Laura (research participant), 34, 72–75, 115, 134*n*38, 143*n*35
lawyers: advice to countersue for sexual violence, 50–51; advice to Marilou McPhedran to settle, 36; advice to refrain from speaking after lawsuit initiated, 11, 66; conduct, 18, 30–34; contact resources, 23–25; financial decision to take a case, 26; opinions on gag orders, 73–74; pro bono counsel or advice, 19, 24–25; in social network, 24; university lawyers, 84. *See also* costs of litigation
Legal Fees Survey, 35
legal limbo, 68
legal settlements, 52, 72, 113, 120; anticipated settlement amount for decision making, 17, 143*n*35; consequences on silence breakers, 64, 72–73; enforcement of settlement, 17; lawyer perspectives, 73–74; settlement meetings, 24, 52, 143*n*35. *See also* gag orders
liar lawsuits, 49
libel. *See* defamation
libel chill (media), 75–78, 117–18
Lucas, R v, 46
Lyncaster v Metro Vancouver Kink Society, 102–4, 116
Lynn (research participant), 3–4, 114–15

Macfarlane, Julie, 79, 89–92, 131*n*51, 147*nn*44–45
Mainstream Canada v Staniford, 58–59
malicious prosecution, 94, 98–100, 114, 150*n*34
Mazhar v Farooqi, 101–2
McGill University, 79–80
McPhedran, Marilou: archive of lawsuit materials, 134*n*33; cost of lawsuit, 36, 78; decision to settle, 36; discovery, 31; *Independent Report of the Special Task Force on Sexual Abuse of Patients by Regulated Health Professionals in Ontario*, 31; opinion piece in *Globe and Mail*, 31, 78; oral discovery,

31–34; Senate bill to prevent using NDAs, 147*n*44; silenced advocacy work, 78; testimony on anti-SLAPP legislation, 95–96

media reporting: advancing stereotypes about women, 8–9, 48; lawsuits against media outlets, 81, 77, 105; of sexual violence, 65–66, 77, 117. *See also* fair comment on a matter of public interest (defence); libel chill (media)

#MeToo, 6, 49, 95, 117, 126*n*2; anti-feminist backlash, 7–8, 49, 86; defamation lawsuits in response, 4, 77; exclusion, 38, 68; male perspectives, 8, 86, 88; research participants' perspectives, 68; silence breakers, 13

Metro Vancouver Kink Society, 102–3. *See also Lyncaster v Metro Vancouver Kink Society*

Morgan (research participant), 18–19, 23–24, 132*n*6

new chastity, 48–49, 138*n*57

Ng v Cg, 100–1

non-disclosure agreements (NDAs). *See* gag orders

Olivia (research participant), 65–66

Ontario Medical Association (OMA), 31–34, 36, 78

peace bonds, 20–21; definition of, 132*n*5; feminist concerns regarding difficulty to obtain, 150*n*31; history of, 149*n*29; in *Rizvee v Newman*, 99, 114

poisoned work environment, 90, 115

police: advocacy to protect police reports from lawsuits, 98, 121–22; assumption that police reports are protection from defamation, vii, 11, 44, 52–54; criminal charges for silence breakers after reporting sexual assault, 3; experiences reporting to police, 3, 10, 25, 52–54, 67, 99–100, 114; misconduct, 94; reluctance to report sexual assault to police, 10, 18, 100, 103; threatened by police after reporting sexual assault, 118; use of criminal defamation, 46. *See also* reporting; sexual assault; unfounded cases

Post, Robert, 45, 60; feminist critiques, 47–48; typologies of reputation in law, 45–47, 60–61

power dynamics: on campus, 81, 83, 85, 86–87, 92, 135*n*54; challenging, 12, 70; in a defamation lawsuit, 17, 28–30, 40, 72, 95, 109, 116, 118, 135*n*54, 140*n*106; men in positions of power, 5–6, 13, 65–66, 77, 90–91; of sexual violence, 120

privilege: absolute, 53–54, 121; in communications, 27; defence, 50; definition, 133*n*24; qualified privilege, 50, 54–57

Protection of Public Participation Act (BC), 98, 133*n*24; difference from Ontario legislation, 149*n*12. *See also* anti-SLAPP legislation; Courts of Justice Act s.137 (ON); SLAPPs

Pruitt, Lisa, 48–49

public interest: legal interpretations, 75–76, 97; sexual and gendered violence as matter of public interest,

99–106, 119. *See also* fair comment on matter of public interest (defence); media reporting; SLAPPs

publication bans: civil proceedings, 37–39; cost for motion, 135*n*50; criminal sexual assault trials, 37, 135*n*44; Supreme Court of Canada, 37

qualified privilege. *See* privilege

racism, 16, 58–59, 81, 114
reporting: definition of, 14; formal reports, 114–15, 130*n*39; workplace reports of sexual violence, 115. *See also* campus sexual violence; media reporting; police; sexual assault; sexual violence
reputation: concept in law, 40, 46–47; damage to silence breakers' reputation, 85–88; as dignity, 46, 60; as gendered, 47–50; as honour, 45; as property, 45–46, 60; protection of, 42; as relational, 43; university reputation, 83, 85
restorative justice, 10, 102–3, 121. *See also* transformative justice
Rimke, Heidi, 62
Rizvee v Newman, 99–102, 114, 150*n*29
Robichaud, Bonnie, 72–73, 75, 115, 143*n*34

sexual assault: criminal trial, 60; definition, 15; statistics, 10. *See also* police; reporting; sexual violence
sexual violence: definition, 15; as gendered, 15–16; legal education, 120; of patients by medical professionals, 96; prevention programs, 83; statistics, 6, 9, 82; stereotypes, 9–10; 34, 121. *See also* campus sexual violence; childhood sexual violence; police; reporting; sexual assault
Shila (research participant), 24, 30, 34
silence: breaking the silence, 12–13; as feature of femininity, 12; silence for protection from legal action, 69–70
silence breakers: definition, 15, 131*n*51; *Time* magazine Person of the Year, 13
silencing sexual violence discourse: fear of speaking about sexual violence due to lawsuit, 4, 12, 68; following #MeToo, 69–70, 77; legal advice to stay silent, 11–12, 66, 116; in media reporting, 75; protection of abusive men, 12; risk of reprivatization of sexual violence, 116; systemic silencing, 12, 116–17. *See also* gag orders; libel chill (media); SLAPPs
slander. *See* defamation
SLAPPs: academic definition, 94; anti-SLAPP legislation generally, 120; British Columbia legislation, 96–97; cost of motion, 109–10; gendered analysis, 95–96, 99, 116, 119; Ontario legislation, 95–97; Quebec legislation, 94, 148*n*6; Supreme Court of Canada, 94, 97–98. *See also* Courts of Justice Act s.137 (ON); Protection of Public Participation Act (BC)
Smith v Nagy, 102–4, 116
social media: attacks on Amber Heard, 5–6; discovery of posts, 107; disrupts hierarchy of content creation, 67; failure of courts to recognize how people communicate

on social media, 58; last resort after formal reporting unavailable, 20–21, 114; #MeToo origins, 126n2; Metro Vancouver Kink Society Facebook page, 102; plaintiff surveillance of silence breakers' accounts, 67–68, 118; plaintiffs naming silence breakers, 37; private settings following lawsuit, 66; removal of posts, 17; to share experiences of sexual violence, 18, 21, 103–4, 114; sued for posting about news story, 57; supportive space for survivors, 67; tool for gender equality, 66–67. *See also* #MeToo

Stuart v Doe, 38, 114

suicide, 52, 65, 88, 107, 119; definition of suicidal ideation, 141n10. *See also* emotional distress

Supreme Court of Canada: on libel chill, 75–76; on publication bans, 37; on reputation, 41, 43–45, 46; on sexual violence, 73; on SLAPPs, 94, 97

Tamara (research participant), 65

Toronto Star, 76–78, 118

transformative justice, 10, 121. *See also* restorative justice

truth, 16; critiques of the defence, 59; difficulty in proving truth, 108; guise of truth seeking, 40; in law, 23, 50–53, 55; of sexual violence claims, vi

unfounded cases, 10, 114

university complaint processes: confidentiality clauses, 82, 88; intersectionality, 82–83; reports against faculty for supporting faculty members, 86–89; retaliatory complaints by abusive men, 83. *See also* campus sexual violence

University of Windsor, 79–80, 90

Vanderkooy v Vanderkooy, 116

vindication: at cost of freedom of expression, 105; plaintiff motivation, 42, 47, 60; of reputation, 42; for silence breakers, 35, 67

Wanda (research participant), 57, 68–70, 75, 108–10, 142n20

Wescott v Wescott, 122

Whitfield v Whitfield, 47, 56–57, 116, 140n106

WIC Radio Ltd v Simpson, 75

Young, Hilary, 110

Printed and bound in Canada by Friesens
Set in Zurich, Univers, and Minion by Apex CoVantage, LLC
Copy editor: Lesley Erickson
Proofreader: Judith Earnshaw
Cover designer: Gerilee McBride